novum **pocket**

AF399634

Julia Tarjan

Growth

novum pocket

All rights of distribution, including via film, radio, and television, photomechanical reproduction, audio storage media, electronic data storage media, and the reprinting of portions of text, are reserved.

Printed in the European Union on environmentally friendly, chlorine- and acid-free paper.

© 2024 novum publishing

ISBN: 978-3-903468-62-7
Cover photo:
Subbotina | Dreamstime.com
Cover design, layout & typesetting:
novum publishing

www.novum-publishing.co.uk

Preface

The bald eagle near the age of 40 flies up on a mountain-top and hits its beak on a rock until it comes off. Then in the following weeks, it eats worms and insects; perhaps another eagle helps it until its new beak grows.

Why is the eagle doing it?

Because if it didn't, within a few years its beak would start to break, and if it loses it naturally, there's no new beak growing. Then the bald eagle would die a long, painful death. But if the beak is torn off by force, before its natural decay, a new one will grow, and the eagle could live for another 40 years.'

What is this book about?

Is it something about nature?

Yes. It's about the nature of our lives; how near the midlife we can find ourselves.

Oftentimes, it comes with huge losses.

My life has turned upside down.

It was a continuous loss; all that I had worked for so hard was gradually vanishing from my hands.

And then, I lost my best friend, the only person who knew who I truly was, my sister.

After that, everything changed.

This is what this book is about.

There are pieces depicting the story of a particular time, in *italics*. In these paragraphs I use altered names in order to protect the rights of the individuals, as all the events mentioned are real.

There are longer pieces that were written at the exact times of their dates. These talk mostly about my thoughts, my understandings, my realisations.

And there are also some poems.

Who is this book for?

Anyone going through a midlife crisis. Anyone knowing suppression of any kind. Anyone of mixed origin or who has emigrated or who has known different cultures.

And anyone open-minded, who is interested in getting to know a particular point of view. That of an Eastern European Muslim woman emigrating with two children, going through grief, divorce, instability, sickness, and healing and finding her soul.

How it started ...

Marina never really grasped it. She came with so much hope into this marriage. Mahmood seemed to be the perfect partner for making everyday life enjoyable; he was fun to be with. And he had a reputation in the community, a respected, responsible position. As much as Marina wanted to find a life partner – that she honestly had much more opportunity for in London than in the small Muslim community of Hungary – she also felt she had a mission. In London, Muslims could eat, could dress, could work, could study, could simply walk on the street without being harassed every single minute. In Hungary, it wasn't so. She wanted to do something about it. And to marry a prominent member of the Muslim community there could give her the opportunity to do something to improve the life of the people. Obviously, she wasn't just thinking about the opportunities; she was a hopeless romantic – that's why she thought she needed a rational reason for her heart's feelings. What she felt deep inside was that Mahmood was a funny, nice guy who would definitely make her happy. So on a beautiful April morning in 2008, only a few years after she had arrived, she left her London life to start a new chapter.

She didn't realise when she understood how wrong she was. The first months he seemed the funny, nice person she thought he was; only a few strange remarks ruined the picture oddly, but everyone can have bad days, can't they? When he put the whole blame for not sorting out the bills on Marina, she felt deep inside he was much weaker than he was showing, and it only filled her with more love and care. Then, when next spring Mageed was born, she was totally drowning in postpartum depression and felt emotionally neglected. But that could be explained away too. Then he spoke a lot about the secretary at the company who even sent her small gifts. He wanted them to get on well. She was a nice girl, sure, but why did he want it so much? Marina had enough friends and that girl did too. Then, the next red flag was their third anniversary. Marina booked a ship hotel; she asked her father to babysit Mageed and was just waiting for Mahmood. He came but called the whole plan off saying he was tired.

The place she felt at home was the Islamic Centre. She led a group of young second generation girls who were the kindest, sweetest creatures. They enjoyed their lessons together where they spoke about the meaning of life and basically everything. She also met a wonderful lady, Beate, a young mother of two of the girls in the group who always cheered her up with her positivity and down-to-earth approach.

But Marina felt she was gradually losing the confidence she had earned while living in London. In Eastern Europe, she had always felt like a fish out of water, but she never thought that after her experiences of living in Italy and the US right after secondary school and in the UK after uni, then marrying a Yemeni, she could forget her power and feel small again. So the plan that she and Mageed spend some time in Yemen with his family came just at the perfect moment. She was excited to discover a new world and she also hoped that she would understand Mahmood more, knowing his family and his culture.

Yemen was a miracle. Marina enjoyed her life as a woman, with all the privileges. She felt like a princess, as if all the bougainvillaea petals on the streets were thrown at her feet deliberately. She learnt *chilax*, chilling and relax, not to worry about a thing, which was a life-changing experience. She studied Arabic, and prepared to start her own clothing company with new-found friends. Mageed went to nursery and he enjoyed it. He learnt Arabic from his cousins in a month and was the favourite of the nursery teachers with his indispensable sunglasses. She went to parties where all the women looked like princesses and all rooted for each other, without competition. She learnt to cook from her mother-in-law who really considered her as her daughter and taught her much more than kitchen pratique. She showed her how to manage a household with no worries, how to not care about what people say, and how to be a strong woman. She also presented how to govern and demand, two things Marina had never seen any example for. She felt good, beautiful, determined. And then, when she finally felt safe, when she finally felt there was nothing wrong with her, she felt a lump in her breast. She had to leave her paradise to get her life.

She had an operation and started chemo in a mountain town in Hungary in 2013. Then radiotherapy in her mother's town. She moved from flat to flat for the whole summer and then to her mother's town in the south where her friend's friend offered her a place to rent. Mahmood was 'shocked', as Dr Asad, her friend and mentor said, and that was the reason he didn't offer her a place to stay right from the time she came back. And then his excuse was that 'she had already managed everything'; obviously, as nothing had been done, she had to do it. Her sister Patricia came from Sweden to take care of her; she brought her two babies with her, and left her school goers with her husband. She stayed for about a month and stood by her in every way. Patricia and their friend Francisca warned her about Mahmood. Dr Asad explained it away, saying her sister was only worried about her and her friend has problems herself, that's why she sees every situation so negatively. This helped Marina keep her pink sunglasses – but definitely wasn't calming to her soul.

Marina started working as a translator, and 1 and a half years after coming back from Yemen, they finally found their flat in the capital with Mahmood. It wasn't the best but was 'just for the time being'. They stayed for 3 years.

Marina worked as a translator online and also at companies as an international communication assistant using English and Italian. She led coffee evenings in the Islamic Centre for converts; they spoke about Islam from a heart–soul point of view. It was her favourite place. They organised summer camps and Ramadan dinners throughout the holy month. Marina was asked by her friend Roxanne if she could join her fashion design project. Marina had studied fashion design as one of her A levels and was always creating dresses for herself, but she had never done it professionally. Her plans for a design firm in Yemen had been cut short by her diagnosis. So now she grabbed the opportunity and they created wonderful outfits for the Budapest Fashion Weeks. Their collections of flowing robes and dresses with turbans and headscarves were a huge success while the country was immersed in fighting against desperate people running for their lives. In Hungary, the 2015 refugee crisis was used by the government as an opportunity to radicalise public opinion against minorities. People who were of visibly different origin or those wearing anything *strange* experienced increasing harassment on the streets. Marina spoke on a morning talk show about the rights of women in Islam – 99 % of the comments labelled her a lunatic. And then, one day, Patricia, from Sweden, found an ad about a secretary opening at the Yemeni Embassy in Hungary. Marina applied and was accepted. In the meantime, she found a beautiful flat and a new school for Mageed. And Mahmood? He realised his long-time dream, owning a company, but struggled to run it – just for the beginning, as every beginning is hard – so Marina's high-end job came at the perfect moment. He didn't seem fully happy though; he felt strange depending more and more on his wife.

Patricia was also diagnosed with breast cancer at the beginning of 2017. They learnt it was genetic. If it had been checked at the time Marina was ill, perhaps … but it hadn't been. She had an operation; chemotherapy and radiotherapy too. For a while it seemed things were going back to normal, but she felt something in her chest. The examinations didn't show anything. Marina visited her in the winter and told her about her concerns with Mahmood who said they might seek a future in Sweden. Patricia said she was welcome anytime. Marina would have loved to live close to Patricia and her family, she enjoyed Sweden, but she felt disappointed by Mahmood's thinking. She had given up her life in London, then she had chosen to stay with him instead of going back to Yemen (OK, the political situation was difficult, but not impossible), and now that she had a good job, he was thinking about living separately again, uprooting her from her comfort zone, just to make it easier for himself.

Mahmood suggested to Marina everyday about leaving her job and working with him in one of his shops. Marina told him she earns much better at the embassy. She also offered to go to Sweden and then he could spend all his money on the shop. But he didn't give up. In the meantime, Patricia's state started to deteriorate; the cancer spread to her lungs and her liver. Mahmood spoke about standing together as a family, putting psychological pressure on Marina every single day. She broke. She resigned from her dream job at the embassy and went to the grocery shop stacking 18 kg banana boxes and dusty potato bags. At first she took the morning shift, but the problem was taking Mageed to school. Mahmood couldn't wake up in time, so she went to the shop at six o'clock, then went home at seven o'clock, woke Mageed up, took him to school, then rushed back to the shop. She did it for a week, but it was a disaster, so she took the afternoon shift – also because others were not able to close the shop in the evening and Mahmood didn't trust his employees. But that meant that Mageed, who was only nine, was at home alone all afternoon and evening. Sometimes he took the tram to come to the shop, but it was dangerous and the shop's storeroom was cold. There was no real place to write homework, let alone to play. Mahmood drove him around by car sometimes but that was not ideal either. Marina's father offered to take care of Mageed every Friday, so at least that day was covered. Her family and friends stepped in too, but the whole situation became more and more unbearable.

And the news about Patricia was getting worse every day.

18.01.19

Marina checks the clock again. 19.27. One and a half hours more suffering. The shop has been empty the past half an hour. She goes back to the store room, pours cold water into the dirty bucket, adds some dish soap to give some impression that it's actually supposed to clean, and starts to mop the brown vinyl. She checks her phone. Patricia still hasn't written. It's been days. The clock is ticking. The floor has dried. Still more than an hour until she can close the shop and go home to her 9 year old, Mageed. She doesn't try to negotiate. Last time she tried, there was a big problem. Like the door. Mahmoud said it should be open. She said it was cold. He said it was only her feeling cold so really it wasn't. Her perceptions don't count.

22.04.19

She is walking slowly to the tube station. She should be in a hurry; some potential buyers are going to see the flat and it should look nice. They couldn't pay for it, so it will be sold. She forgot to take enough banana boxes for their stuff. Maybe tomorrow, but she doesn't like to go to the shop. She spent too much time there when she should have stayed with Patricia. Mahmoud left the day after she came back from her funeral. He went to find new opportunities as his business was about to collapse. Marina should hurry but she just can't. Anaemia. That's what the haematologist said. And she had nearly fainted (not her, the anaemic pregnant woman, but the young and healthy doctor) when she had told her about her family's medical history. The baby should be fine. She had discovered she was pregnant in the fifth month. She had never thought it was possible, but she had been worried all of the time about Patricia, Mageed, and the situation. She feels he is fine now. But he is taking every bit of the scarce nutrients she had taken in the past half year so she is just left there with nearly nothing. Starving in a grocery shop! How ironic!

25.05.19

Marina and Mageed are sitting on the train. Her father Joseph and his wife Lia offered to drive them, but they wanted to take so many things so, in the end, there was no room for them in the car, even though it was just the most necessary. The rest of their stuff is in the cellar of the cultural centre. They will get those posted to England to them once they are settled, probably around October. She is happy. This is the first step of their emigration she is telling her son. She just needs to give birth, get a little strength, the baby too, and they can fly away to their new life.

Marina is in the hospital. Linden fragrance spreads in the whole area, and from the window, if she could stand up, she would be able to see the flat her sister Patricia and her family used to live in. If she could stand up. She cannot, actually. Little Yunus is in her hands. Beautiful! With those tiny little eyes, he is looking at the world like a wise man. And those feet! Strange shaped and purple! Granny and Mageed are coming in the afternoon. And the person from the council is coming too; hopefully, he accepts the paper from the embassy. Otherwise, his name will be Jonas in the documents, as Yunus is not on the country's official given names list. Mahmood hasn't sorted out the paperwork so Yunus will get her family name. What a shame! As if she wasn't married. He is saying it doesn't matter, but they know the truth. Marina thinks it does, but what can she do? Anyway, there is this sweet baby here now and she just wants to focus on the good things. The following months are only about relaxation and full dedication to her children.

The taxi stops in front of a council block. Marina saves the driver's number, as he said he might have a flat to rent later. It might be useful, but for now, Jasmin has welcomed them into their spare room. Jasmine and her family received the council flat after she told Marina that they could stay with them until they got settled. Another woman in Scotland did the same, and she received her council flat too soon afterwards. Marina chose this opportunity as Walsall was still closer to London, her long-forgotten dream city – and now they are one step closer!

Back to writing – back to life
09.11.19

As the mermaid is back to her sea, she can sing again. After years of silence, here I am again to share my world with you. This time not *somewhere far in the south* though – too many sharks. I am in the foggy Albion, which suits my mood more for now.

It is not easy to emigrate. We know from family chronicles that my great auntie was washing dishes for 5 years before she could finally work in her field as a ballet teacher when she arrived in West Germany at the age of forty. As Ginger Rogers did everything that Fred Astaire did – backwards, in stilettos – so I'm emigrating with a 10 year old and a 4 month old.

Why am I doing it? Why am I taking the pain of insecurity, waiting for months for basic things like a school or a proper home? Of course, it is for my children's future, but really it might have been more rationalistic to wait for another year for better circumstances. But there was this drive that ejected us from Hungary and it grew even stronger with the baby.

That evening, the refreshing Swedish air touched my face. I knew I was home. As Massimo di Cataldo said over 25 years ago, '*Perché dovunque vai non sei straniero mai se hai la tua casa in te,*' – wherever you go, you are no stranger if you have your home inside you. I have it now alhamduliLlah. My home is inside me whether I'm in Sweden or in Italy, the US or Yemen, London or Paris. Everywhere.

But not in Hungary.

It's not right to depend on ... anything. How can I let a country, especially the one I was born and raised in, stop me from being myself? What is this deeply grounded block that didn't let me live my life not only in that society but also among those who are the closest to me?

And why was I silent during all these years?

The situation is very serious back there.

My mind instantly switched to emergency mode. A red light flashed, a siren shouted big problems.

Lots of people are involved.

I cannot help.

The only way to help is to not create more problems.

Not to ask for anything.

Not to have a voice.

Not to have needs.

Not to be visible.

Not.

To.

Be.

...

To disappear quietly as a tree in the forest.

Subhan Allah.

At a certain step of my healing process, I realised I was not the patterns I learnt. I nearly died unlearning them. Not all of us are that fortunate.

One thing everyone should consider when entering a big family one way or another, is that overwriting personality issues is one thing, but I should also learn to take my own place and not follow the hidden written family dynamics with the same role.

That place doesn't belong to me. It was my elephant rope. But I'm big now, I can walk away. No one is forcing me to think I don't need anything.

I'm not small. I do have needs. I'm taking my place under the sun. For me and my sons.

It might be far from where I was born. It may also be far from the one who did not see behind my words. It's not his fault. And not my fault either. Nor of those who taught me the best they could. Everybody carries their own burdens.

But not those of others.

I have my needs and take them. My non-existence would not benefit anyone. My existence does. My shine does.

I will shine for all those who still feel they are not allowed to. I will find my way.

For she did not disappear among the trees of the forest. Her example shines above the sunlit snowfields. Above the silhouettes holding each other on that ice-cold clear afternoon. She showed us an example of living and loving until your last breath.

This legacy keeps me going.

Mageed is at school, and on Yunus' fifth month-day, Marina signed the contract of a one bedroom flat on the top floor of a house. She also found work as an admin of a lifestyle magazine online, so it's just perfect with the baby. And the British state calculates benefits in a rather generous and reasonable way, at least coming from a place that doesn't care how people survive, that's what it feels. Marina's Eastern European heart is grateful even to the Asda self-checkout that thanks her after each scanned item. They sleep on an old mattress, but they finally have a place they can call home.

25.04.20

The little flat is getting nicer and more comfortable month after month. Marina first bought a used fridge, so they didn't have to keep milk and cheese in the bathroom window – well, with the arrival of spring it was high time. Then as lockdown hits, they order a nice double bed and a chest of drawers from Ikea for Mageed. Now the bedroom, where they spent the winter all together, becomes his territory, and Marina and Yunus occupy the living room. Marina bought 6 metres of pink velvet at the high street market when it was still open and she created a pair of curtains with the help of safety pins. She also found a very comfy armchair in Cancer Research for £5, they delivered for another fiver. She found a mirror in their backyard, so both rooms look homey.

And Yunus is happy in the baby chairs and baskets they got from Jasmin.

Something else happened on a beautiful pink dawn. After so many years of suffering, Marina finally felt peace. She couldn't explain it in any more a rationalistic way than feeling God's love and acceptance. And it meant that anything that would require her to give herself up was not love. Now she knows.

Her marriage is over.

Getting cold
02.06.20

When people are asked
To give up dreaming
They are usually compensated
By some lukewarm stability
A life without poetry
Tasteless with no fragrance
Yet a life worthy of lying
At least for the outside world
A golden cage they say
But I was required
To cut my wings
Only to sit in a cage
Made of old wires
Where I had to search
Food for myself
And after everything
Has fallen apart
Dreams awakened from deep inside
And I'm ready to fly

25.07.20

They are on the bus, going back to their hotel from Jeannette's house in East London. It's their second getaway in London, the first since travel was allowed again. Mahmood is coming. She has been waiting for him for more than a year, for 10 months since they arrived. She had told Jasmine back in November she felt the time was approaching when her patience would be over. Then that pink morning in April, when she felt she could be loved … whatever it was, it was true. And there was no way back. She told them it was over. Then Jeannette and Sunny told her that Mahmood was interested in that other girl and continuously asking Sunny about her straight after he married her. They told her after she told them about her decision. And now he is here, waiting for them at their hotel, their so far peaceful cove. Yunus will see his father for the first time. Mageed after nearly 1 and a half years.

10.09.20

Mahmood cooked, took the kids to the playground, and went with them to Ikea. Marina said if the past 10 years had been like this, now she wouldn't have made this decision. But they hadn't been. They are trying to behave like a family for the kids. Yunus loves him immediately; Mageed, now 11, finds a new connection. Marina is saying they could be friends, but nothing more. He is nice. Now. They go to restaurants and parks. Then to Hungary together – but he stays with his relatives and she with hers. He signs the official fatherhood paper; Yunus finally has his real family name. Mahmood is trying. Saying he is coming back. If he really had … if he had rented a flat in London, started working there … he really would have had a chance. But he doesn't come back. After spending 2 weeks with them, he stays in Eastern Europe for another 6. Well, what does Marina expect? It has always been like that. She doesn't want to wait for her turn again, being the last on his list.

21.10.20

Marina announced to the community, to Dr Asad, that she wanted to divorce back in May, after the end of Ramadan. Then Mahmood came in the summer, so everyone hoped things were back to as they were before. But they weren't. Marina knows what she wants but no one stands by her. She has strong grounds – he was supporting them less and less even while they were living in Hungary. He lost the flat and didn't provide any living opportunity; she had to go back to her Mum's place to give birth because the flat had been sold before it. Then all the way she was emigrating, he didn't support them 'because he was building his new life in another country and every beginning is hard'. She has heard that already.

But she is not feeling heard. The community doesn't set up a meeting between her, Mahmood, Dr Asad, and the religious leader where things can be discussed openly. Are women's rights only on paper?

**Different approaches
27.10.20**

There are people
Who won't listen to you for years
The only time they do
Is when they feel
They are losing you
Or better say
Losing their influence over you
But even if they listen
They won't understand
Who you are
They only talk about themselves
And there are people
Who listen to you
Even when you are silent
Who remember
Every single word you said
When you didn't even realise
They were around
Who understand
Your unspoken words
Who feel
Your deepest emotions
Who know you
Under your skin

Eastern European Muslim
08.11.20

I'm done with the whole issue. I recognised it and will not let it control me anymore. Mother wound, Eastern Europe, narcissistic relationship, and all their support system. The vested interests of patriarchy masquerading themselves as the noblest healing methods of spirit and body. Doctors swear to save lives, not to stick to protocols even if it means death, and every path to God considers the human and their rights.

The underlying thought of every such harm is that you need to give yourself up in order to be accepted. And the trap is always there: even if you give yourself up, it will never be enough. You will not be loved, not have a place in society, not get any guarantees for healing and so on.

Why?

Because acceptance is never conditional. A newborn child needs to be loved just the way they are. Not if they sleep all night, not if they don't cry a lot, not if they can be left alone for long. They need to be shown that their needs are important, otherwise something will break inside them. If their needs are not met, they will feel they are not good enough. They will try to change in order to get the love they crave – but there is no such love. A parent who has unnatural expectations will never be perfectly satisfied no matter what their child does. Even if they do the very thing that's expected of them. And the same is true about an unfair society – you can work day and night, but at some point you will find yourself exhausted and excluded; or about a narcissistic partner – you can forget about all your dreams, you will be left with nothing. And then you will believe that following the doctor's advice all the time will surely save you, while they only follow protocol, and in the case where it's not working for you, they don't even say sorry. And if you try to get justice, you are told to wait until you change your mind, and anyway, your problem is not that bad as no one is really getting hurt. And you wait and trust the system as you think at least you are safe.

You are not safe if you trust anything or anyone that has ever made you feel you are not enough.

If you are not enough for a person or a system, no matter what you do, you will never be enough. Don't trust them, don't try to seek their approval, twisting yourself and turning into something different. You can dance on your head, but they will never appreciate it and will still blame you for not trying harder.

And as long as you believe them, you will always blame yourself and forget about your own feelings, your own personal power and everything magical you are.

And … that's the whole point.

Once you know who you are, you stop seeking other people's approval.

You will set your boundaries to those who always know better.

You will find your own way inside the society – and recognise if it means that you need to leave.

You will not tolerate being used.

You will listen to your instincts.

You will seek your own justice.

You will be empowered by the fact that you will write your own story.

Maybe
02.11.20

Maybe I should
Really bury
My feelings
Deep inside
They are so tiny
Like the cells
Deep down
But actually
They are
The very cells
Of which
I am put together
So sorry
But no sorry
This time
I'm not going to
Give up
On myself

Heart and soul
13.11.20

There is probably no more widely discussed topic in Islam by Muslims than the question of Istikhara. It may be because this supplication is about the greatest issues of life, the biggest decisions one has to make, and it involves the heart, mind, and soul.

Istikhara is a short supplication one says after a voluntary prayer asking God for guidance by His knowledge. After praising the Creator for His all-encompassing knowledge, the supplicant asks Him to make the issue easy and bless it in case it's the right thing regarding this life and the next, but in case it's not, then distance it from them and them from it and show them what the best is.

All clear so far. The hard part comes after: how do we know the result of the Istikhara? How do we know which way to choose so that both God is pleased with us and we don't feel we are being pressured?

There are many ways of interpreting different levels of authenticity that I don't want to go into the details of as it's not my field. Some say you will have a special feeling, even a dream, and you will know in your heart firmly the right thing to do.

But what if you don't have any feelings like that?

Then you should use your utmost ability to reason, consider every possibility from every angle and make a decision. If that's not the right thing God chose for you, don't worry, it will become impossible. The Creator and

Sustainer of the universe won't let you do something wrong after you have asked for His guidance.

I have recently heard another interpretation of the issue that says: if you want something but it is increasingly becoming hard, it might be a sign of the issue being the wrong decision. Although I don't doubt the credibility and authenticity of this interpretation because of the sound knowledge of the people mentioning it, the topic triggered some deeper emotions inside me.

Every great achievement in the history of humankind was something difficult. There was the hero who had a dream, who was surrounded by a little group of supporters and a great crowd of people who thought they were mad/insane/unfit/obsessed/a troublemaker/scandalous or all of the above. But they still went and did it – and made history. That's true about geographical discoveries and scientific inventions, and Islamic history is also full of such events for that matter.

We can mention human development as well; giving birth is a struggle in itself, and whenever the child is learning something new, they keep trying until they succeed. No child thinks, *Walking is not really for me*, after they stumble for the hundredth time. They get up and keep going.

Fine. So we can conclude that the fact that something is hard does not necessarily mean that it is the wrong decision.

Yet a scholar and a very knowledgeable friend mentioned that when we find something very hard, it may be a sign of the issue being the opposite of what God likes.

But were they talking about my case?

How is *very hard* manifesting in my case?

Is it oceans I need to cross without the sure knowledge of whether or not I end up in a bottomless abyss?

Is it a human being I need to push out of my body causing unbearable pain to myself with every move?

Is it the divine truth I found, a burning love in my heart and soul that I want to share with my people who hate me and hurt me for it?

Actually, none of these. I have only mentioned my feelings shyly to two people; the position of one of them makes it impossible for him to agree with me, and the duty of the other person is to try to discourage every such situation. So they – as expected – didn't clap their hands for joy when I mentioned my wish, didn't facilitate any step forward in the issue, and would not talk about it if I didn't.

Is this the hardship that's the sign of God's disapproval?

I don't think so.

It's definitely a sign – as many things are – but this sign refers more to me than to the situation I'm in.

I mentioned children learning to walk. When did I stop that? I mean, I'm walking, sure, thank God, but when did I stop working for my dreams?

I have always been a dreamer.

And I can also say, many of my dreams came true. Not the way they appeared in front of me at first, but the essence of them.

I was always told not to dream. I could blame my parents or the society for it, but that's all they knew. They said I need to concentrate on the facts, on the opportunities, and leave my dreams behind. I could never do it. I lived my everyday life, doing my duties, but my heart and soul were absent – so I never actually became successful. I had one reality for my dreams and one for my everyday life. In my dreams I was in magical sunny places and met wonderful people and worked on interesting projects, while I considered my everyday life a sentence, living in survival mode. I have actually never fought for my dreams. Never even knew I could. It's not a new thing for me, it's just the first time I have realised that I have never considered my dreams as valuable starting points I should count when planning for my future. They stayed in the air, suspended, as a cloud following me and giving me some fresh oxygen sometimes when I'm about to suffocate from my everyday routine.

Then one day, the routine everyday struggle became impossible. The carpet had been pulled from under our feet and I told my son, 'This is the first day of our emigration.' We only went to a different town, yet we emigrated a few months later – accomplishing my dream from childhood. But it wasn't planned; it was just a necessary step for our life.

My dream is less and less cloud-like. I sit down quietly and listen to my soul. I close my eyes and see my heart. I pay attention to my inner voice – something that has always been there, neglected and silenced. But never killed. I could never be the person who can be successful using only their minds and physical abilities. Silencing my heart and soul only made me handicapped, paralysed, half a person. I have always felt something is wrong with me – this is why.

I will embrace my whole being from now on – my mind, my body, my heart, and my soul. I want to give all of these parts their rights.

People who knew me may be surprised. They may not understand what's going on, so they cannot help and support me. What I really need is to support myself. I know what I'm doing, I know why I'm doing it, so I need to stand by myself. If I don't do it, I would betray myself again and I can't afford that anymore. Not now that I know about it.

I have a dream and I have made it a plan, creating a roadmap towards it. I will go step by step through it and will reach it with the support of God. I will take along my heart and my soul, freed from their prison, enjoying the sunshine of reality. I will take care of them and never let myself or anyone treat them wrong. This is my responsibility.

Ultimatum
17.11.20

People keep telling me that I should have given him an ultimatum. Told him that unless he sends me a certain amount every month or rents a flat for us by a certain deadline, I will divorce him. Of course it also means that if he is able to meet the requirements, I will go back to him, living with him as his wife, trusting and loving him as if nothing has happened.

How much am I supposed to sell myself for?

How much does my trust, hope, and love cost?

If he manages to get the amount by the deadline, will that erase every feeling of being neglected and used? Will that build my trust back up after all that I have gone through? Will it create love after I tried to believe in it long after the very end, and letting it go was the only way out?

If I still believe that we can have a future together, if I trust him, there are no ultimatums. I will stand by him in good and bad times. I will wait patiently no matter how long it takes.

That's what I have done so far.

I didn't give ultimatums when there was still a way back. I stood there with all I have. I gave my time and money, my attention and dedication, my trust and love. When my life turned upside down, I still searched for the 700th excuse and made plans for a future together.

Then one day I couldn't do it anymore.

Trust crashed under the weight of lengthy disregard and the whole story started to make more sense without my explanations.

I said it's over when it was. Without trust, love died and there was no way back.

You tell me to give an ultimatum.

I can't do it.

My love doesn't have a price.

Long recovery
07.12.20

I have recovered from COVID. Yes, I don't have a fever anymore, I don't cough often, and I can even smell my baby's nappy.

However, recovering from chronic fatigue, anxiety, and my inability to focus will take more time. COVID attacks the weak points of the body. I am healing step by step from PTSD. I am discovering the symptoms and effects of it day by day. By the way, it is actually PTS, not PTSD, as experiencing stress as a result of a trauma is not a disorder. It means you have a healthy way of thinking.

One such effect I have just discovered is the moment I have been deprived of my womanhood. Strange enough, it happened only a few months or weeks after my marriage, in a rather intimate situation. My husband practically said that I was not interesting as I am. Of course he sugar-coated it in a joke, but something broke inside me. I was not the woman he was blown away from. He had previously played to me the most romantic song, he wrote me poetry, inspired lines, and talked to me every day for months. Yet when I left my promising future and chose him over my life in London, he was fantasising about others.

From that moment on, I stopped being a woman. I became his servant, trying to please him in every way.

I felt wanting something different from what he wants would be a tragedy. I wasn't strong enough to take a stand against him. And I think he knew that. I was fighting, but not against him, against myself. And the result was what I called *complicity*. I felt that was the solution to keep him: if I can't be the love of his life, I'll be his best pal, his good friend he can tell everything to. And that's what I became – just to be with him.

So we became *halal friends with extras* and we would have had a great marriage as such – if I didn't have a heart and a soul that was starving.

But I only know it now.

Then I struggled to keep my feeling of being neglected down and took his physical closeness as my regular dose of emotional security and reassurance of being loved.

Then God took this drug away from me.

It was difficult and I went through all the phases. I was blaming everyone else, though inside somewhere I felt I wasn't right. I was fantasising about him coming back, but it was totally away from any sort of reality. I still wanted to keep the facade of this non-existent marriage in front of others and ourselves but it became less and less possible. To create a new home and security for my baby and my adolescent was hard enough, I couldn't carry more burden.

Step by step I started to allow myself to be angry with him. There was no point in pretending anymore. Until one pink morning in a blessed month I decided to put down this burden. I saw myself and I realised how alien this life I had been living was.

Now I just want to breathe fresh air into my lungs. To see the colours of the sky. To hear the singing of the birds. To laugh carelessly. To dream and to make it come true. To dance to my favourite tunes.

And not to walk on eggshells.

03.01.21

The process is not going anywhere. Back home they are just waiting for something. At the London Religious Council there's no one to answer the phone. Maisa, the downstairs neighbour, suggests the former religious leader. He seems promising, then disappears. Marina feels anxious. She is taking nice walks, taking care of the kids, understands more and more of herself, her soul that had been chained long ago in a mouldy cellar. She sets her free, washing her wounds. She tells her it's all right, she will take care of her from now on. She walks with Yunus in the red pram. She prefers the vegan diet, and tries to live healthily. But the situation worries her and she doesn't see a way out. Is it possible that a woman who has every reason to ask for a divorce just can't get it done? Why does she need to be tied to a man who is not providing anything for her? Who actually never understood her and never took her as a priority?

It's been 2 years …
02.02.21

The day you left
I understood
This life is not
What we hoped for
This world is now
An empty place
It's so hard to
Be in peace
I can never
Talk to you
I can never
Share with you
All the heartbreak
And the joy
All the things I
Got to know
I want to tell you
Since you left
Everything has changed
No way back
Illusions faded
And new rays of
Hope are shining
Through the mess
I will miss our
Endless talks

Your special ways of
Making jokes
Deep, understanding,
Caring heart and
Your bright soul that
Lives for God

Narcissistic discussion
06.02.21

The past months I have participated in many groups about the topic of narcissism and I can only talk about positive experiences.

These groups never aimed to substitute knowledge or therapy, but they provide excellent support. I don't mean I talk to random strangers and cry my problems out, but if I read about events that are similar to those I have gone through, if I discover that the actions of others towards me are typical examples among the characteristics of a certain disorder, it helps me understand my feelings. Reading it shows me that my experiences are real, my perceptions are valid. It is already a step away from the effects of gaslighting. Empathy warms my soul after long years of isolation. I did have people around, even close friends, but I have never allowed them to see certain parts of my life – in fact, I have never allowed that to myself either. I couldn't face that walking on eggshells had become my actual way of walking. Now I'm discovering step by step the effects of narcissistic behaviour and know that others have been there; that all of it is real, frees me.

I do go to therapy and do my research on the topic. I could not do without it; I would not have gotten this far without it. I do need to hear the professional explanation of the issue, but my main concern is my own healing. And part of my healing process is to have my experiences acknowledged by the world. To know that all my doubts, all my sensations that something fundamental was missing, were not my own paranoia, but I was right. This behaviour is not unique, it's not caused by me or my own behaviour learnt from my past experiences, but it's a real, existing textbook-proven way of an actual personality disorder.

To understand how someone's personality is affected and what percentage they have of a certain disorder, if any, is of course impossible through the accounts of others, even by the best of psychologists. So obviously, to know if someone else can be labelled as *narcissistic* is close to impossible as it's them who need to go to therapy to be diagnosed, and even if they went, it's very unlikely that they would share the diagnosis with you.

But to talk about my experiences doesn't mean that I'm labelling anyone. To understand through psychological counselling and literature the type of trauma that I have gone through is not equal to and not aimed at diagnosing other people without having a PhD in psychology. The whole issue is not about others but about me, my own feelings, my own experiences, and my own healing.

And to acknowledge what I feel, to own my experiences and to be able to heal, I don't need to have a PhD. I just need to be who I am.

I recently read a comment on the topic of narcissism that made me think a lot. It confronted personal experience to professional diagnostic work where these two are in completely different areas and never meant to substitute one for another. The former was in a way dismissed, comparing it to a much simpler issue. Reading this was painful as it reached the very point inside me that was hurt for years. Not because of childhood traumas but because someone systematically eroded my relationship with and my perception of my senses. And to call a possible narcissistic behaviour a simple communication misunderstanding reminds me of the gaslighting I suffered from for all those years.

It's painful also because I thought the same way. If I heal from my own issues, so will the relationship. There is no such thing as a *bad man* who is responsible for every one of our problems. He's not an angel, true, but not a devil either. I needed to find out what our relationship could become once I was healed from my own traumatic experiences.

Well, I did find out.

This is what it can become.

There are people that are just like a bottomless well. If you pour little, little will be lost. If you then pour your best, all of your efforts into every single level, that will also disappear without any sign.

After years of experience, it took another while to be able to face the problem at hand. No one played with the gaslight switch anymore and my eyes started to see the things for what they were. And what I found, the psychologist called it, the 'behaviour of a person possibly having characteristics on the narcissism spectrum'.

In fact they were exactly that even many years ago – when I was trying to convince my friends and myself that it was only communication issues and my own personal unprocessed trauma.

This was my path. I didn't lose these years, I needed them to know it 100 %, and I couldn't have realised it earlier because of the very nature and extent of the trap. But now I'm out. The nightmare ended. No one will ever explain to me anymore that the sky is green or the grass is red. I'm breathing fresh air now and learning to believe and acknowledge what my senses are telling me.

Dependency
13.02.21

All my life I was afraid of dependency. I wanted to avoid it at any cost. Most probably I felt that way because I had seen my mother collapse when my father left her who she depended on emotionally, economically, existentially. I wanted to be myself, determining my personality without the influence of anyone else. I know you need to be able to ice skate alone so you can dance with someone else who can ice skate alone. I just didn't know how to do that. And I was even less able to spot the red flags and the signs that would tell me that I was about to be captured.

I always thought that my wish to travel was a dependency. I felt that if I go somewhere and I feel happy, confident, determined, then it must be an outer factor making me that way, because when I'm *at home*, I become irritated, moody, depressed, indecisive, and passive again. I thought that's what I am as that's how I have always known myself.

Years passed and I discovered more and more places, looking at more and more different mirrors. The interesting thing was that no matter where these mirrors were from, I continued to see the same woman: she is full of ideas and willpower, she is funny, she is a mediator, a facilitator, she is ready to learn new things and to share everything she knows, she is able to show the world who she is. Not someone living on low flame. Not ashamed of being herself. Not a violet under the bushes waiting to be discovered.

Although I understood that the places I have lived at were very different, the fact that I have always known who I was in the east and west, in the north and south, but never in the land I was born – that by the way never felt like my home – just never made sense to me. I have known it's like this but I could never explain why. I knew that when I was a child, I copied my mother, and then when I was married, I unknowingly played the same part, but I knew it was only a part of the issue, it's about something more complex.

A few days ago I was talking to a friend about this. I told her that as I'm getting near the end of my marriage, I feel excited and interestingly whole. Like I am complete the way I am and I'm not in need of anyone to complete me. As I was talking to her, the realisation came: I was not dependent on being in Italy and in the US and in London and in Yemen and in Sweden and in Walsall. I was, and I am, being freed.

I was dependent while I was living in Hungary. I looked at myself in that distorted mirror and I saw myself as small, quiet, begging – no, sorry, quietly waiting – for love and appreciation. I saw someone who didn't know what she wanted, who depended on the way others looked at her. That it was a dependent state of someone walking on eggshells, being constantly careful not to make too many waves. That behaviour I have learnt since childhood was a dependency and it continued in my marriage – not because I chose something familiar, but because I had no idea what was going to happen.

I ended up in a dependency in order to recognise the pattern and then end it completely.

I know now who I am not. And who am I? The most interesting discoveries are there in front of me! What I know about her so far is really interesting.

3 days
16.02.21

3 days
They asked me 3 days to reconsider
No compulsion, they said
Then mentioned my children
While they know
Or they don't?
Yes, they must be perfectly aware
That there isn't stronger compulsion for a mother
Than her children
So 3 more days to reconsider
But I'm done with thinking
And explaining
And reasoning
And mentioning my rights
Everything is ticked
Yet the pressure did not end
It became stronger instead
And got trickier and stickier
Using my own dreams
Against my own willpower
Painting beautiful pictures in front of my eyes
Of a life I once dreamed of
Mentioning an ideal situation
I spent a decade
Pretending to be living in
Hiding from everyone and from myself the fact

That I was not
3 days
I'm fasting
Not eating
Not drinking
Not speaking
Not reasoning
Just being
I let this river take me
I surrender
To the Lord of this river
And of every being
As I know He won't let my heart bleed
And will take me
Where I really belong

What have we done to Islam?
20.02.21

I am a revert myself, so some of the statements implicitly portraying me as an ambassador of the religion may seem a bit schizophrenic, but I will explain.

I became Muslim in my early twenties after a childhood and teenage years that left a lot of blank spaces in my book of *how to live*. So my personality was shaped largely by it as in many areas Islam was the first guidance I found after wandering around blindly. It was the light in the darkness, the meaning after the confusion, the roadmap towards a meaningful life. I studied it day and night; it became my primary interest and I implemented its teachings in my inner and outer actions.

We lived in an ideal small community. An Eastern European university town where many students from Muslim majority countries had chosen Islam after being confronted by the life without it and discovering the differences between the cultural customs of their countries and the religion itself, and open-minded reverts, many of them uni students as well, who were eager to learn everything about this complete new lifestyle. We studied about rights and duties, about ways to get closer to God and nice manners to facilitate our relationship with other people, and learnt how to respect ourselves and each other. We built lifetime friendships; we became each other's real sisters and brothers. This was our refuge.

Years passed. We all got married, had kids, and focused on personal careers. Everyone moved out of town; community life was concentrated at the capital where there were more people ... But focus was lost somehow.

Studying Islam didn't mean learning a new way of life that makes sense and is liberating but to listen to lectures – through translation – about a bunch of rules and old stories with very little explanation. New reverts' hands are not held, the organisation body is solid as a rock, and we simply lost the second generation.

What happened? What did we do? How did we end up here?

Islam is a comfortable Yemeni sofa or an ergonomic chair, it's a cosy house designed to have room for everyone. We made it into a concrete structure with sharp-edged walls and the threat of dark abysses you may fall into if you are tired of sitting on the cold and wet ground.

We, all of us, used to stick to the divine word. There were no cultural differences; it did not matter where you were from or how long you had embraced Islam for or what the norm was in your country because we all wanted to follow the guidance of God. We felt we managed to escape the trap of culturalism many Muslim diasporas had fallen into. Now some people – many in responsible positions – just tend to create their country here. They guard rules but they forget they can't replicate the whole society. You can't expect children to be respectful and obedient without giving them the security of an extended family and set of neighbours, or even the people on the street who would surround them with love and reassurance. You can't expect reverts to follow every rule if you don't want to understand them, you don't explain to them in a way you make sure they understand them; plus, you never even intend to give them a support system, without which their rights will simply stay as words.

We have also fallen into the trap of culturalism, and a culture, even the best one in its own place, will never be the answer for the second and third generation or those looking for the truth from elsewhere.

Why do we think that if we keep criticising young people for not praying enough, not memorising enough Qur'an, not speaking enough Arabic, not dressing modest enough, not behaving decent enough, they will like and follow these things while society is criticising them for the opposite? Why don't we simply show them an example of what Islam is like and why don't we give them a shelter against outside criticism? How do we expect them to choose the path we show them, sorry, speak about?

We should go back to the basics. We should try to implement the teachings of Islam in our daily lives, in our dealings with young people and reverts, and basically everyone. Our families. Ourselves. Think about the rights they owe you. And if we really want to create a small Yemen here, bring the sunshine. The softness. The smiles. The taste of tea. Then, and only then, will we be successful in our dawa.

What have we done to marriage?
23.02.21

I believe in matches made in heaven and soul mates. I know that somewhere there is someone for everyone who can be just the perfect companion for them, who can understand and share their weirdness – as everyone is weird in a certain way – but for *the one*, these things are perfectly normal. It's a connection that involves the heart, soul, and body; it's as if there are millions of microscopic strings pulling them towards each other constantly.

I also know that it's not guaranteed for anyone to meet their type of weirdo in their 20s, or if they do, they are not guaranteed to recognise each other and be at the point in their lives that they can start their journey together. So yes, it does happen that soul mates don't meet or don't recognise each other until they are in their 40s or even later. If it was so, and if all the people waited for their soul mates to arrive finally from the desert or from the depths of country life, this world would be underpopulated within a few decades.

There is another way, and I don't even say it's less in any way. People could also get married to others who are not necessarily their soul mates; to a nice person who is willing to do everything to make it work. These are the matches made on earth, and they require a lot of openness and honesty to build a common area. The couple needs to be equally committed in their relationship, building it step by step, brick by brick, channelling every resource towards this common ground. If they are able to look each other in the eyes to get to know who they really are, they will discover a new universe and will build their love every day.

This can happen if it's all built on honesty and willingness to give from both sides. If, however, one of them has other intentions, if they weaponise the closeness of the other in order to get something from them, if they're not willing to give from their hearts, just counting and measuring the amount of time, money, and emotions so as not to give an extra second more than necessary, then it's not real marriage for me, it's something else.

And if the community encourages this, it's a disaster.

What do you think about students who are only preparing for a pass mark? Are they committed? Will they ever read about the subject after the exams? Do they care? Is it their favourite subject, or just something they need to pass in order to reach their real goals that are different from the subject in question?

Allah set up boundaries. These are the limits, the borders of a deed being accepted. We need to know them in order to stay between them whenever we have no more energy or capacity to strive for more. Let's take the example of prayer. We generally try to do the sunnah prayers to get Allah's rewards, a palace in Jannah if someone prays 12 extra rakat every day, but if you are at work and have only limited minutes of breaktime, or you have a baby and you hardly know if it's morning or evening as you are stuck between diapers and breastfeeding, or you are just simply tired today, then you only do the fard ones, as that's the minimum obligation. But once you are back in your normal state, you will strive for more as you do care and you want the reward of Allah.

Well, rewards are there in so many actions, but people forget that.

You might also go for only five prayers if you are a new revert or a young person and the whole issue is still new for you. But some years later when the love of doing something Allah likes will be stronger in your heart than the trouble of some extra concentration, you will want to do more.

I could bring endless examples: from a person who loves their job and thinks about new solutions even while on holiday to a runner who gets up every morning to do their training and will do some extra rounds after finishing because they know that's how they will win and so on. The point is the same: if you are committed to something, if you understand by your heart and mind the positive result of it, you will never stop at the minimum, at the pass mark, but will try to do more and more.

Likewise, if you are not very young or new to the concept, and your minimal effort is not temporary, it very simply means that you just don't care.

What is this whole discussion about?

Well, how many times have we heard things like, 'She has never asked for more time/money, so he doesn't need to bother', or 'A husband only needs to stay with his wife at night, so what's her problem', or 'Her father's (temporary rented) apartment (where he only stays for a few months) has older furniture so this apartment (furnished with used furniture) is just right for her'. We have accepted the fact that men are only required to aim for the minimum when it comes to marriage. In their job they need to be the top dogs, in the mosque they need to be the first line of Qiyam, in society they need to be the most generous, but when it comes to their wives, if they sleep at home and give them minimal financial support, they are considered to be perfect husbands. If she has a roof above her, he is a very nice person, if she doesn't, he is still 'not a bad man'. Spending time with family is not necessary, there are the grandparents or her friends for her as company. Spending time with her only is considered an unnecessary woman's romantic thing she nags for; remembering anniversaries or her birthday is not his culture and, by the way, not even Islamic, and actually, the Prophet SAS never gave his wives roses (well, husbands of this type never run races with their wives or repair their own clothes for the record, but anyway ...)

So this, marriage today, the way it is tolerated, portrayed, introduced, taught in many mosques, gives licence to men to act as if it is not a priority, and conditions women to accept this.

The problem with this (among the host of others that psychologists and sociologists could write books about) is that it is nothing else but a set time bomb. Times are different according to the individual levels of abuse (emotional neglect IS abuse) and the extent of pre-conditioning of the suppression of wives, but sooner or later, most women will have enough of it and they will leave.

It is also unfortunate that this is the example children see and grow up with, and it is possible that they will follow it in their own families.

We need to go back to the basics. Marriage is one of the most important things in this life. It is the foundation of society, the cradle of the new generation. It's where people learn to be humans, where the right characteristics are implanted; it is the place of emotional nutrition we take with us through our lives. We do need to take it as a priority, and when it comes to priorities, you don't check the pass marks, you go for the maximum. As with every goal, you will not always score. Sometimes you will, but other times you will go lower, but this is still OK if you aim for the best.

What happens when your goal is to pass? You will, for a while. Maybe you get some help, but your ego prevents you from facing it; you are still there, everything is fine. But one day you wake up and you realise it's over. And that's when you understand that your efforts were not enough. Or ... you may not realise that. Good luck then.

Fears and finding my soul
17.03.21

More than twenty years ago, I spent one of my most self-defining years in Italy. I was a volunteer at a country hostel, helping a lot in the kitchen – that's where I first learnt to cook. I didn't only learn the recipes but also that you need to add a pinch of love to every dish, as the cook was an extraordinary lady. Whoever she looked at, she saw their hearts.

Once a guest entered the kitchen asking about lunch. They started talking and after two minutes, she had told him the major events of her whole life in a nutshell. He left and I looked at her astonished. 'How could you do that?' I asked.

'What?' She didn't quite understand what I found strange about her behaviour. Then I explained to her that my first thought about sharing anything about my life is that people would judge it; they would have negative opinions about it and about me in general. Now she was surprised. 'Why would anyone think anything bad about you?'

Then and there, being eighteen, drying my shrunken wings in the sun for the first time, I answered her, 'Really, why would they? Surely, they wouldn't.'

It wasn't until I got back to the place where I grew up that I realised where that fear was coming from.

An interesting feeling has run through me recently that opened my eyes to further aspects of being Eastern European.

I usually don't share my plans with many people. It may be a type of trauma response – I know I wouldn't get real help, emotional support, or useful advice, only misunderstanding and degrading, condescending negativity.

I checked myself: I really had no problem with people expressing their views that are different from mine. Everyone's free to do that. If it's about my life and they are telling me the only possible right choice while considering my life plan as something inherently stupid, then in that case, it's a bit harder to be tolerant and acceptive. I still understand though that people are different, times are different, cultures are different, and if you were born and raised in a dictatorship, you can't help but think there's only one good solution for every situation. I still don't really understand why people trouble themselves with creating scenarios for others on how to live their lives, but again, it has nothing to do with me.

What I really got scared of was my own reaction.

An otherwise very nice and understanding close person told me – without me asking their opinion – that what I had been planning the past 3 years, considering firstly others' interests, is simply pointless. This put me in a position of being thoughtless and even irresponsible. I felt weak and confused.

I started questioning myself and those in my life as to whether it was really the best thing for them. They confirmed, but I remained hesitant.

I felt I needed to explain myself, and that I would not be successful if I didn't get others' approval.

At this point I stopped.

Really?

Where is this fear coming from?

It must be some very deep childhood feeling since a small child really cannot live if they are not accepted, approved of, appreciated, and loved. And for that, they will do everything. Even denying their own needs. Even saying no to what they feel is right.

There we are.

No.

Not anymore.

This is my life. I have my children in it whom I would do everything for.

I have my own experiences.

Everybody told me not to go to Italy, to come back from the US, to stay away from people of different cultures, not to become a Muslim, not to go to London, not to get married to the one I chose (even if it didn't last forever; at that time, that was my decision and I respect that); then they told me not to go to Yemen, and later, not to come here, and not to divorce.

I did all these because I could not find peace not doing them.

If I wanted people's approval, I would not be myself.

When I wanted people's approval, I wasn't myself.

When I believed people's fears and explanations, I thought with only my mind and it didn't make sense. Everything was *rationalistic* yet it didn't feel right.

That was the same rationalisation I used to silence my inner voice when I felt something was not right, but I stayed and looked for the 777th excuse.

I don't do that anymore.

For my own safety and sanity I will not leave my own heart and soul out of the equation. They have a say in my decisions, in my life, in my future.

My heart had been hurt, and I felt inferior, lacking love and acceptance. So I did everything to be acceptable – betraying my heart and soul by it.

About my soul, I didn't recognise its voice for so long. I didn't know that the tiny yet strong feeling, when you know the truth, is actually the voice of your soul, worth listening to.

Being accepted and doing the right thing: these were the two things I had felt long ago. I gave up the second to get the first. I didn't know it was the other way around.

I need to listen to my soul and do what it tells me. Then my heart will be at peace too, as I'm accepting myself.

Only this way can any kind of suppression end.

Freeing your soul
20.03.21

I understood the whole picture I guess …

About heart and soul and the rest.

Your soul is you.

That was chained and blindfolded and closed into a cold and wet cellar.

Not by your parents – I mean most probably they led you and chained you there, but not because they were bad people, just because they were slaves and were doing everything following orders.

Their souls are also chained in other mouldy cellars and are most probably dead now – even if they are still around.

The system they grew up in made slaves of them by depriving them of their ability to choose between right and wrong, to recognise the truth and everything that belongs to them. It killed their souls.

They were left crying, hungry, wet, and cold so they learnt to neglect their senses. They are aliens in their bodies.

They are not shown love; they were gaslit into believing that they were not lovable. That made them beg for love and acceptance in exchange for anything they had. They were made to feel that in order to be given a right to exist, they should sacrifice anything that's required. That broke their hearts.

They were also given a whole ideology of rationalisation that explains how they are not right in every case. That confused and corrupted their minds.

I have never known my soul.

It was only a few times that I felt what was right and I knew what I wanted to do.

Most of the time I acted from my broken heart begging for acceptance and ready to sacrifice my dreams. I filled my heart with the world, with others who I thought belonged there as my soul was still tied and blindfolded, so I could not listen to it. I didn't even know that was an option. I didn't know until a few days ago that I have something inside me; a compass that could guide me to everything that belongs to me.

I knew what I liked but was always miserable as I depended on them. I felt my happiness was conditional to getting certain things, and when I didn't, I just felt left behind.

On the other hand, I was always ready to sacrifice my dreams. I felt if I didn't go out following them, it would be good for others. Wanting something was considered selfish.

This all put too much weight on my heart as it was also acting instead of my soul that was still in chains.

I didn't know there are things, places, people that belong to me. I always felt the things I liked were different from me, and that I needed to do something to get them. But the truth is that they are a part of me. It was my soul that was screaming to me from the cellar that I should finally listen and recognise them. They are not alien to me. They are not something I need to buy for my precious time or money or body or by not following my dreams. They are my dreams. They are me.

But I need my soul to recognise them.

If it's something you can't get out of your head and your bones, if it's everywhere you look, if it's the first thing you think in the morning and the thing that makes you sleep like a baby, then you know a part of you. And even more importantly, you have found your soul.

Free it from the shackles. Listen to its voice and believe that no matter what, these things, culture, music, people, etc., are part of your life. They are inalienable to you and it's only a question of time for you to be united with your missing parts. And the soul knows no time.

By the recognition and freedom of your soul, your heart will be freed of the extra load it had to carry all along. Your heart is actually the place of love towards someone you are not.

Your Creator.

In the remembrance of Allah do hearts find rest. It's true. But to be honest, as long as we trouble our hearts with all the burdens of other people, our own wishes, and the dreams we believe we need to sacrifice in order to be accepted by society and everything else, there's actually no more room for the One who created it.

But our hearts are free now, not needing to play the part of our souls.

So your heart is for your Creator.

And your soul and everyone and everything in it belong to you. They are you. Free your soul. Listen to it. Trust it as it is telling you the deepest truth there is.

By freeing, listening to, and being guided by your soul, your heart can find peace loving its Creator, and your mind will also not be bothered by confusing ideas. It will be free to think, to learn, to create.

And your body will also heal, as it's the manifestation of all the rest – if that's its destiny.

This way we can live the way we are created.

Your heart will be filled with love and gratitude towards your Creator for everything He has done to you and made you understand.

And your soul will shine bright, showing your way through this world and leading you towards its unalienable missing pieces. They are your home in this world and the next, they are your family and everything you like and feel familiar with. You are right. You have always been.

Follow your soul and it will lead you home to your family.

Acknowledging our state
31.03.21

Many times when I talk to people who suffered from dictatorial abuse, after they have been familiar with the problem itself, they blame themselves for their behaviour or actions, even though these are the direct consequences of the issue. They may say things like, 'I was so stupid putting myself last', or 'How could I believe it to those who didn't understand me?' and so on.

Knowing now what would have been the best way then is already a great step forward.

We also need to accept that at a particular point in the past, we did not have the knowledge and ability to behave that way.

We need to go back to our soul and understand the phase we were in at the time.

Most probably we were still tied up and blindfolded in the wet cellar.

Would we question anyone in that state why they couldn't dance pirouettes?

If we blame our soul, we will be on the side of the suppressors. They make the soul unable to do it right, then accuse us for it. Pure cruelty.

What can we do instead?

In order to heal our souls, we need to acknowledge that the pain is valid, the hurt is real. We have to allow ourselves to be imperfect. Yes, we were not able to act in the best possible way, not only because we had less experience than now, but also because of the effect of the suppression and abuse we suffered. We cannot accept one without the other. If we state that there has been suppression, we have to let go of the expectation that we should be perfect. We are not, just as any human being is not perfect, plus we need to face our vulnerability and the fact that we are hurt. It is, by the way, one of the tools of the suppressors that first they hurt you, and then they accuse and blame you for being hurt.

What we need is a protective atmosphere for our souls to heal. To acknowledge the negative consequences of the suppression, to believe that you have suffered, to check the extent of the damage is one of the very first steps in the healing process.

We said we need to caress our souls, and we should care for their wounds. How could we do that while expecting them to be perfect?

They are not.

We are not.

And to face it is the first step in the process of healing our souls.

Permanent victims
01.04.21 (no joke though)

Abu Hurayrah (may Allah be pleased with him) reported that the Messenger of Allah (may Allah's peace and blessings be upon him) said, 'A strong believer is better and dearer to Allah than a weak believer, and there is good in both. Adhere to whatever brings you benefit, seek the help of Allah, and do not feel helpless. If something befalls you, do not say, "Had I done such-and-such, it would be such-and-such." Indeed, *if* opens the way before the devil to act.'

Sahih/Authentic. [Muslim]

In another translation it doesn't say 'don't feel helpless' but 'don't stand there with your hands tied'.

I imagined it as wearing a straitjacket.

How many times do we feel like that? There is no way to do anything, all the options are impossible, we just don't really have a choice.

It also comes from society. If you have always experienced situations in your studies, in your family, in the workplace, etc., that your wishes are practically impossible to come true, and instead, you are left to choose between bad and worse, it's obvious that you learn this is how life is.

It is also a very natural and rightful reaction of your soul to all the negativity it has ever met. Of course, the soul feels victimised as unlawful things were done against them that were never corrected, never apologised for, and never even acknowledged.

But our soul that possesses the sense of justice feels that it's just not how it should be.

There are two types of victims:

Everyone is against me, or

God punishes me rightfully, as I am/have done something wrong.

We know the mind cure of both. We explain to ourselves or our brothers/sisters that Allah SWT is Just; whatever befalls humans in this life is not a punishment, but either an atonement or simply a blessing as it will draw more reward in the Hereafter. We can also tell them this is the nature of this life: bad things do happen to good people, and it's not THEM it's only happening to, look at this or that person, how bad they have it.

We can remind them of every good and sublime thing we have studied in Islam and it's all good and beneficial.

But it's not enough.

Feeling like a victim is a symptom.

A symptom of our soul being neglected, traumatised, not defended, deeply hurt, and all that has never been addressed and treated.

Only if this is done will our permanent victim feeling end.

Then there will still be situations that trigger our dark memories. But we will know it's time to go, not to stay. The most important thing in these cases is to recognise the difference between the victim feelings originating from childhood neglect and institutional suppression and the fact that this world is not a fairy tale.

This latter fact has nothing to do with you. It's just the nature of it. This life on earth is not meant to be perfect. No matter what you do or what is done for you, no matter your background or your efforts, many things are going to work out and others will not. It can be finances, people, health, anything. You have no total control over your life, you just have to accept that, and build a large and thick wall between these problems and the deprived feelings of childhood

as that is a totally different story.

That needs to be addressed properly and this too.

It's not, it's never that, 'I got these problems in my life because I'm such a loser and I can never get anything right.' That kind of feeling only shows that childhood deprivation has never been treated.

And when it's not treated properly, then all the *mind cures* will become toxic. That's why we talk about *toxic positivity* or *religious mind-police* because we use these tools, these remedies, at the wrong times. We use them for broken people.

People who have their souls in chains, who feel they are bad but also feel it is unfair to be called that, who have never ever experienced unconditional love and acceptance or, if they did, they pushed it far away as they didn't know what to do with it, who only know rejection and degradation and walking on eggshells as human interaction – these people can't really make a use of sublime spiritual teachings.

These timeless wisdoms may sound no better to victims of soul enslavement than just another standard they need to follow, just another set of outer requirements they need to meet, obviously focusing on the outside, and then eventually when they get tired of it or realise how far it is from their soul, they start revolting against it as if that was the worst tyranny they have ever experienced.

How many times have we seen this?

And there's nothing to be surprised about and there is even less to judge. To teach some of these things is an enormous responsibility. You don't only have to learn the language of these people but you must be aware of their socio-cultural backgrounds. It's not enough to ask them. Read their literature, learn their history, walk on the streets, look into their eyes. Are they calm? Or fearful? Do they trust you easily? And if you have done all that, remind them that the thing you are teaching them is suitable for those with healthy souls. If any of it feels like oppression, then first they should heal their souls. You can also help them by showing unconditional acceptance, but it's not certain to work out well. And it's surely not enough.

And us, victims of oppression and neglect, we owe ourselves that cure for our souls. It is not something we *have to* do to meet some outside requirement. We need it because we need it. Let us let our love free for ourselves. Let's listen to our souls about this oppression that happened. It is a valid reason to be hurt. We should go deep in it and we should give ourselves consolation about it. We should do everything we need to in order to feel better and feel complete.

This is the step we can't miss out on. It must come before all the smart dos and don'ts. So let's just breathe and relax a bit.

Last third of Ramadan
05.05.21

As we enter the last third of Ramadan, the heaviness this Ramadan brought has vanished and has been replaced by a new force of doing all possible. This Ramadan has been the most difficult so far of all the 19 years with late hours, my son also fasting, and morning school runs.

Or maybe because I have realised that life is not a creamy cake I had one Ramadan. I was pregnant with severe iron deficiency so obviously I didn't fast, and last year Ramadan was in lockdown, and it was all about discovering how easy life could be, with the pink morning sky, when I felt real, unconditional love ...

But now here we are, with my adolescent complaining about Ramadan being a race with time with no time to relax and why Allah wants us to suffer, and I know it's not the point, but I also find it difficult to feel the sweetness of Ramadan like all the previous years, when I lived my life in a comfortable lukewarm lie, which was increasingly becoming uncomfortable and cold.

Then after *loss of lives, wealth, and fruits*, I found myself sitting with my childhood friends as the reality shocked us all: this world is not a walk in the park for anyone. You will surely suffer, and life is not like how we dreamed it when we were adolescents.

You will be neglected for years, used and abused, and then left in the middle of nowhere, or conditioned to give up what's the most valuable thing and not to aim higher than your own fears, or continuously living in emotional and physical pain, or trapped in a set of self-contradictory explanations, or told that any difficulty this world brings is a consequence of following your heart.

And you accept and serve your sentence. You get up every day and go out in the rain and wind, you fight with your utmost energy for those who depend on you, you go and never stop, never give up, no matter how scary and grey your surroundings are. You know this life is a constant fight and not a fairytale. You fight because this is the nature of things.

And then the last third of Ramadan comes. The nights when you can ask anything. Anything.

And suddenly things make sense.

When we were young, we dreamed dreams and thought that's what life will be.

Then we hit hard ground and understood that we will not sit in a country villa in the south of France with my sisters in this life. It is just not the place for that.

This is not a resting place but a testing place.

But not the place of sentences either. Not even of useless suffering.

We are here to do something. And we can't wait for anyone to do it for us. If there's some help, it's fine, but not necessary. It's our life. We have got to do the best with it. We have Allah. That's what's needed. Our love and trust in Him alone. He is the Only One who will surely treat our issues with due improvement and nothing is lost that's trusted to His care.

This is a new level of لا إله إلا الله. Not to expect people to treat you like family. Even if they are. Even if they make everyone believe they will. They will let you down.

Just like Yasmin Mogahed and the vases. They will break. And by doing so, they break your heart too.

The heart is only for Allah. It should not break, so it has to be attached to the One who won't break it for sure.

I understood that so far … but I felt lonely and cold. I still needed people, but those I chose by mind hurt me in unexplainable ways.

I felt like a zombie and no wonder why.

My soul was still in chains.

And without a soul, with a broken heart, one is a zombie.

My heart, my trust, my dependence is totally for Allah. I don't expect anyone to solve my problems but Him.

And my soul is free, I'm freeing it, caring for it step by step, healing its wounds. It's sitting still at the shore, having survived the shipwreck. It is just alive. Breathing.

One day it will be the leader. And now it's ready to explore the world.

Walthamstow
20.05.21

Everything is growing. New, modern houses emerge from places where there was once nothing but rubble. Old houses are being renewed by their new owners who appreciate their values – you see mosaic doorways, colourful front door windows, sophisticated colour paints, and terracotta vases by the doors.

It's the same place yet the air talks about new life here. It was once a dirty suburb – now it is a modern residential area for families and professionals where they can plan their future.

The place has not stayed the way it was long ago. It managed to take the tide and transform itself into a new quality. It did get outside help (the nearby Olympics nearly a decade ago poured new investment into the area) but it didn't stop there. Walthamstow reinvented itself as a new centre of humane living for all. Multicultural, definitely, but it's not even an issue anymore. It's for the people.

How did it happen? How did this dirty, boring, sometimes even depressing area, become a cool place to live?

It seems like it has taken its values seriously. It looked inside and found all the different positive features its diverse people carry. And then it used them to grow.

When I'm walking in Walthamstow, I feel like I'm young. I left this place 13 years ago but walking down the same streets makes me feel like time has disappeared. I'm full of energy, and everything is possible in my life.

Yet Walthamstow is different now. It didn't let itself be determined by its past. It is a modern place now that is proud of its own ways and values.

It also resonates with my life.

I'm who I was before: the young girl who came here to build her own life. But I am now a strong woman who would never give herself up for whatever nice promises she gets. I have looked inside myself and discovered every different value I found along my path and I am willing to construct a future for those who belong to me. I am enough as a home for my children and I am not shaken by outside danger.

I am Walthamstow. My home is inside me.

18.06.21

She is in the fortress park she used to meet Patricia in so often. She would ride a bike and arrive taking one of the girls with a radiant smile on her beautiful face.

Then, years later, Marina walked this path carrying new life in her belly, little Yunus. And now here she is – carrying death. The fast-growing hard thing is bigger than a baby's head. It is a tumour, starting from her ovaries. Dr Asad, her teacher, mentor, friend for so long, was trying to make her accept that the kids would be fine with Mahmood. That's what he could say. Nothing like, 'Don't worry, it's going to be all right.' After seeing what happened to Patricia, no one has any hopes left. Mahmood signs the divorce papers. It doesn't matter anymore. Something she has fought for desperately for more than a year is now granted, or better said, thrown at her. There you go. You are free now, anyway, there's no hope for you.

Yunus is two. Her friend Mandana throws a wonderful party for him. He doesn't understand anything, where they are, who all these people are, why they can't go home, why Mom cannot hold him. He holds onto Granny. Mageed's world collapses too. His dreams, his hopes all vanish into nothing.

Marina only arrived in Hungary for the midterm break. She scheduled this checkup at the hospital where Yunus was born because in Walsall it was hard even to get to the GP and she needs yearly checkups. She thought there might be some hernia that was hard, but the news of cancer arrived as an ice-cold shower.

No more plans for summer visiting the cousins in Sweden. No more hopes of moving to London. No more stability. No more life.

What should she do?

If she went back immediately, it might still take months to be seen by the doctor. And she would be alone.

Should she stay? Here is her mum, her friends, the children are safe … but what about financial stability?

The most important thing at this moment is to be treated as soon as possible. The town has a world famous gynaecological oncology centre, doctors are looking for connections to get there soon (yes, that's the way you can be treated in Hungary …).

This seems to be the safest for the moment.

New life
03.07.21

It's time to rewrite history.

I arrived at the end of May from a place where I was happy and strong.

Getting the diagnosis that doesn't only change the plans for the following months but might as well include deadly danger.

I froze from fear.

It's all too similar. Except that now it's much more serious.

A rollercoaster of events. The life I had built up step by step is taken away from me, one by one. My health, my plans, my trusted source of support. I'm in a whirlwind and barely have time for desperation.

It is a force much stronger than I could control. I cry, I try to hold on for a while, but it's so overwhelming that, honestly, I can only admire it.

If a sickness returns, the reality is that it has never healed completely.

The trauma response I gave last time was not effective for my healing.

It was the way I got sick.

I was the good little girl trying to please everyone in order to be accepted and thus gain her right to exist.

Having my health, my life being threatened by a sickness, I went back to my familiar way to cope and to survive, trying twice as much to be the good little girl, annihilating my needs and my personality, existing only to serve others.

That's what I had learnt as a child: that's how I behave in my marriage, accepting the unacceptable, and thus became sick, and that's what I continued to do after my sickness, watching my oxygen being gradually taken away.

And that's how I became sick the second time, which was, according to the above-mentioned theory, my first sickness I have never been healed of.

So now it's time to heal.

Really.

Thoroughly.

Not only from cancer.

From the good girl syndrome.

From annihilating myself to accommodate others.

From denying my dreams, my desires, myself.

The change had already started when I first stepped up for myself and for those who belong to me. I decided that I would not live the life of a victim.

I won't back up.

I will go on and won't stop until my life is as it was in the vision God showed me as a promise.

I surrender to His plans and accept all trials during the process.

But I won't surrender to the creation.

Not anymore.

Pain in my soul
17.07.21

Tumours form from the unlistened feelings and emotions inside us.

I have just started to discover the process of freeing my soul from the chains of the suppressive society and embracing her with all the pain she is bearing. Washing her wounds gently, taming her slowly, step by step, to learn about being loved.

What is she trying to tell me?

A friend, a sister who has already walked through the path of this sickness before, shared her insights with me. We both realised that cancer came at a point where, although under different circumstances, the *good girl syndrome* was not sustainable anymore.

She spoke to me about how to heal. To be determined and to choose healing. To choose life. To choose the future. To choose life and everything in it. Indeed, to make choices every single day and to declare fearlessly who you are.

She also said that she heard somewhere that to forgive and not to hold grudges against anyone frees you as anger hurts and destroys you more.

I listened to her in awe, drinking in her words as a source of life – until the last sentence. A sudden pain cramped my stomach and my body froze.

'But it's about injustice,; I said.

'You don't have to hate the sinner, but the sin they did, it can provoke anger. The concept "to hate for God, for justice" exists.'

She got it.

I got it too, very deeply. I got this unexpressed anger towards everything that ever made me small. That told me to wait quietly until my time comes, but it never came. I believed that I had to silence myself and my feelings in order to be accepted and then, one day, what I wanted might happen.

This happened in my childhood, in my marriage, in the divorce process, and even during the organisation of my medical treatment.

I always had to be patient, considerate towards others' feelings, expecting the best and explaining the 777th fault. I had to forgive and forget and let go. Others' mistakes are human flaws, but mine are to be dwelled upon for years and characterised basically all the behaviour towards me the following years.

My feelings are invalidated, questioned, and swiped off the ground. Yet I'm expected to be strong, nice, and unhurt. If I mention something that hurt me in clearly vulnerable situations, I'm called inconsiderate. For having human feelings. Or for being cold. Or for worrying about my rights. And about my life.

All of these are bright examples of patriarchal systems, of misogynistic behaviour.

It's when women are told to accept it, accept it, even if it hurts.

It's when women are told to 'have patience' while patience can never mean to tolerate deliberate injustice.

It's when divorce is made so difficult that it's almost impossible, no matter the circumstances.

It's when in blatant cases of carelessness and neglect, the right of the one who did it is much more important, since he 'didn't mean it'and 'is not a bad man', than that of those who were left without anything.

It is when the noblest teachings are twisted and turned to serve men's comfort only.

Yes. All those things anger me.

And what makes me sick is not my anger but that it was silenced for so long.

I want to go out into the rain and shout it all out. Or to dance a haka, a South Pacific warrior dance. To tell all women that you don't have to let it be done to you. That's not piety. That's not sabr (patience, perseverance). That won't make you a better servant of God. On the contrary, it will make you a servant to unjust and oppressive humans who might look the best to the society, but God knows about their hearts.

I want to articulate that this is not right.

I do hate this injustice. And I know it doesn't make me a bad person. Accepting injustice would.

And I know that it doesn't make me sick to express my anger towards injustice. Silencing it did.

I also know that writing this article won't make any difference in the everyday practices of many people and institutions.

Even if it reached them, even if I told them to their faces, it would never happen that they stop, think deeply about it, and then they say sorry (unless it's a personal situation – been there and recognised it right in time as yet another attempt to gain influence).

So after all these words, nothing will change, right?

People who hurt me will continue their lives as they did.

I can tell my friends, other women in similar situations; they may smile between their tears, making their beautiful eyes even more sweet, but unfortunately, this article cannot give them enough force they need to fly away from their not so golden cages.

Why bother myself with this then?

Why focus on negative things now when I need to concentrate on life and health and beauty and friendship and family and love – things that, thank God, my life is now about.

I am focusing on the positives. I am inexplicably grateful to God for surrounding me with such wonderful people. And then I am grateful to these wonderful people who think about me, pray for me, and support me in every way they can.

But I owe this to myself. To listen to me. To my hurt soul. To the little girl in the corner who is still waiting there for someone to hug her and play with her because she was good and quiet. Who was then acknowledged as an easy child who doesn't need anything. And to the young woman who thought marrying based on a mind decision will save her from heartbreak. Who kept quiet and wasn't complaining, and was, consequently, acknowledged as an easy task. I owe it to the pregnant lady who was worried about her other child at home alone while she was carrying heavy boxes and her senses were questioned. And who, a few months later was forced to leave her apartment and give birth alone, also being denied of her dignity to give her son his rightful name. Who fought and settled with her adolescent and her baby in a foreign country. And who, when following a wonderful vision, finally wanting her rights back, was continuously silenced, emotionally manipulated, avoided, mansplained, etc., for over a whole long year.

I owe it to you, my dear self.

I'm here now. It's all right now. Just cry, the clouds are crying with you too.

What happened to you was very wrong.

And yes, bad things are part of life, but if we see something bad, we should change it by our hands; if we can't, then by our words, and if we can't do even that, by our hearts, meaning that we have to call the bad things by their names inside our thoughts. That's what our religion teaches.

But we were told instead to call the wrong right, to think about negative things as positive, in a way that was messing with our perception and taking advantage of the innocent optimism and the virtue of positive expectations.

No darling. You can say it now. I can hear you, my dear sister, my soul.

Dimension gate
24.07.21

The wounds hit by the dimension gate
Are deep in my stomach
I'm laying down motionless
Trying to perceive every single piece of my aching body
And grateful soul
I'm alive
Thank God
I survived crossing the stargate
However I have suffered serious injuries
Due to the nuclear explosion during crossing through
But I'm here now
On the other side
I'm in my new life
On the path of full trust in God
And total acknowledgement of myself
I will fly like never before
Just like a phoenix

My soul, the queen
25.07.21

What my passage is about, not only the words but also this chapter in my life, is freeing my soul. One's soul is one's real self that senses oneself, understands their role in the world, and recognises the things it belongs to. Even though my parents did everything they could to raise us with love and support and care, they were themselves children who grew up in a dictatorial system. And a dictatorship destroys souls because that's how it can control the masses, as if they are soulless zombies blindly following orders. That's how children are raised or, better said, trained, from kindergarten in these countries. So I didn't have connections to my soul as it was closed inside a dark room. I had a very close connection to places and people that reminded me of my soul. Italy, the south of France, Yemen, and, first and foremost, my sister. I think it was the moment I lost her that catapulted me into a space where I had no reference point. There was no one who knew who I was, only some parts of me.

I have started to reconnect with old friends ever since. This process had already started before, as Allah knew what would happen.

I never actually knew 'what I wanted to do when I grow up'. I did many things, I gave my all doing them, but I eventually felt burnt out as I never felt they were my mission, my ikigai. No wonder, as one's ideal job, their mission, also belongs to the soul.

I had the same cluelessness about finding my significant other. Back in the days of ignorance, I chose by my eyes. A complete disaster. Later, when I was smarter, I chose by my head. But there are features no checklist can filter out and no trusted friend can warn you from. More than a decade later, the disaster was even bigger. None of them were my soulmate. But how could you possibly meet your soulmate if you haven't met your soul? Even if you do, you won't recognise them …

I'm reconnecting to my soul now. She won't be banished anymore into that wet cellar. My body is her rightful estate. No matter that it started to decay as a body without a soul is in fact dead. But now, as my dear sister Mesi sings, it is rebirth. My soul takes back her reign as the legitimate Queen of Julia Marina Country.

My body is the country, my soul is its queen, my heart is its prime minister, and my mind is its executive officer. The country is ravaged by wars but with the ruling of the once-exiled queen, it will be whole again very soon ان شاء الله يا رب.

This is where my inner feeling of being of nobility deprived of my rank might come from. It is part of family history, but I felt this really close.

This is what Najwa Zebian called being your own home. My soul is being reinstated in her reign. And the country will be rebuilt by the grace of The King of Kings.

Marina is in her bed. She spent 3 days in the hospital. They were trying to operate on her, but it was impossible. Laparoscopic surgery had been performed to see what the situation was. The tumour has spread around all her belly, and also around her intestines. It is basically impossible to cut it out now. She needs chemotherapy to get it reduced. The tumour produces water – she remembers how much Patricia had suffered from it – and it is reduced during the operation, but within a few days it's back as before. Three huge wounds are emitting a strange fluid. She is slowly healing from them but the tumour needs an immediate solution – and it's not coming.

The missing link
10.08.21

As I have mentioned earlier in the blog, shortly after I got my diagnosis, I ended up in a very low place spiritually. A person who is of course not perfect, to whom I will always be grateful for teaching me so much and whom I respect a lot, told me, most probably to make me less worried in an already difficult situation, that we can't be more merciful than God, so I shouldn't worry about the future of my children whatever happens.

It put me in a position where I felt that life goes on with or without me and there was basically no need for me to fight for my health. Allah deals with everything and everybody better than I, so I should not stand in the way.

Later I managed to gather up my pieces and was able to pray for healing as a special gift or favour from God, as He is The Most Kind, The Most Merciful, and He is Able to do all things. So I begged Him to save me, even though there's no need for me, and there are so many more terrible things happening to people; that's the real nature of this life, but as He can, and only He SWT can save me, I asked him to do it.

Nowadays, as I'm finding my way back to myself, just like in Ramadan or in other blessed times when we forget about our fears and write to our long lost friends and we can talk for hours as if all those years we were in our lonely towers hadn't existed, my old friends find me. And yes, we continue as if we just stopped talking yesterday. A friend of mine wrote to me who I have always thought about, but we just haven't written across the years. Both of us have gone through a lot these past years and have grown. She is now the same age as I was when we had a group of young girls whom I mentored in the mosque. Every time I think about them I smile, it was a very beautiful time for me.

She told me to remind myself of who I was. And yes, she did ma sha Allah. She pronounced the most basic, yet most important principle of our religion. I remember teaching them this. There is even a paper picture of me wearing an old fashioned brown Asian qameez and writing on the whiteboard of the old mosque *intention*. One of the most important and basic teachings of our religion is that deeds are according to our intentions. The definition of a good deed is if it is done for God, and in accordance with His laws. My friend, my former student, told me that I should fight for health for God. So simple! And so far I have not understood it. I have not done it. Somehow I got the concept that fighting for my health would mean not accepting God's order and rebelling against it.

There must be some very deep inner fear that traumatised and paralysed my soul by linking fighting for life to a rebellion against the order. It tells me to be quiet and wait passively for my fate, whatever it is. If I stand up and go, if I search for opportunities for myself, this force reprimands my soul for not waiting patiently. My former mentor's innocent suggestion opened the door to a very dark abyss – the one where my little dear soul was chained for years and decades.

My sweet soul! It's all right now. Life is a beautiful place. It's still waiting for you to discover it. Go ahead and live! Heal! Fight! Work hard for your dreams! Talk about your experiences and thoughts! Go ahead and love, drive, breathe, swim, ride horses, take care of your dear babies and your sister's babies, and make every one of your dreams come true!

By doing so, you are not rebelling against the order of the universe. Your role in this whole beautiful symphony is not a tree that disappears in between the millions of others in the forest. Your mission, assigned to you by the Lord of the worlds at the moment of your creation, is something extraordinary. Something that you still need to do and to share with the world. It requires a lot of strength, courage, confidence, and trust in God. You possess all those qualities. Come to the light, my dear soul! Your Creator wants you to try. And He promised you something beautiful ...

I couldn't fight for my life and my health for God because under the surface there was something telling me that passivity is a *good thing*. It's the right thing to do. I'm a good girl if I sit around and wait quietly. How long have I been living like that? Basically, all my life up to this point! I did many things, but in a shy way, not my way. I tried many things and then backed up, so as not to make too many water circles. I did everything quietly, never too loud, so as not to disturb people. I travelled and came back, I started projects and stopped at the first obstacle, I learnt and never used it, I made my way through new circumstances and then changed my mind and never went back. And I felt and then ran back to safe destruction ...

Time to rewrite history, as I have said before. The whole of it. This is what this sickness is there for: to teach me. Because my plans, my goals, my dreams cannot be fulfilled working only in second gear for them, we need full gas now. A full tank of determination, love, strength, and courage, used properly. I possess all these qualities. And the voice that makes me sit down quietly is just as much a liar as the one that told Van Gogh that he couldn't paint. His answer was right: just go on and paint!

God doesn't expect me to be a passive spectator of my life and the loss of it. He wants me to fight for it and every beautiful thing He has promised me. Now it's time to learn to walk again – literally. And to fight. And to do so for God. For His sake and pleasure, not for anyone to see me and to have any opinion about me. That will be a secondary side effect. One day I will talk to people about my whole experience.

This is what shows passivity cannot be ordered by God – it cannot be done for God, only for people. God likes the doers, the rebels, the ones who went against society's conventional habits. Actually, every prophet was a revolutionary.

I'm now going to start a revolution against passive life and old fear that comes from generations. I will live on my own terms. And I will do it for God Who likes innovators.

I can fight for my life and work for my dreams for Allah. So can you.

13.08.21

Marina doesn't look like herself. Her face is grey-yellow, very thin. Her beautiful dark eyes are sunken and have so many wrinkles around; they shine with a strange colour from a different world. She still tries to smile in the pictures. Her arms and legs are skinny and weak. She can't take a shower alone. In fact, she can hardly sit up. The tumour and the water it produces takes all the energy out of her. It's not a cooperating lump, like a baby. It's hard and wants her body all for itself. Or it could be all her unlistened to pains incarnated. People come to visit her and cry.

She gets her first chemotherapy on the 17th of August. The last moment.

The experienced doctor who has seen a lot, gets scared because of how she looks.

Female power
01.09.21

The first time I recognised it was at the birth of my second child. I had a female doctor back with my first delivery too, but that was completely different. I felt I surrendered to outer forces. My husband at my head telling me which supplications to say and my doctor, an older, respectable lady, at my legs, telling me when to breathe and to push. And there I was, in the middle, just following orders while an immeasurable pain was tearing me apart.

It was followed by two years of untreated depression and utter emotional neglect, and my only happiness was the smile of my child.

My second baby was born in a very different way.

I was alone. My then soon (well, officially two more years) to be ex-husband had already been gone for months and I had to leave the apartment we were living in. We moved to a southern town to my mother's small house and I gave birth in a country hospital where I knew the head of the neonatology and paediatric departments. That was a privilege, but without a husband, without the name of my child, I definitely didn't have a position to envy.

My doctor was a woman about my age. She was nice and practical. The nurse was still in her 20s, with no child of her own. I had problems with contractions, but since I had diabetes and because of my age (41), there was no time to wait. I got oxytocin and step by step I was getting there. The morning of the delivery was overwhelming. I tried sitting on a ball, but then I realised the baby was coming. I felt every contraction and I owned them. My doctor was very enthusiastic, she was breathing and crying with me. When I had a problem, she responded to it immediately. She didn't rule the scene, she was aiding and supporting me. I did everything there, I had my pains and I responded to them. I felt my body getting ready for pushing. One huge effort – and he was out. My sweet baby who had no name, no father, but who was looking at the world with curiosity from the first moment.

It was a very empowering experience. I can do this alone, I can do it better than before.

Now I'm getting treated for cancer. From the gynaecology department there was one young female doctor who finally cared about my case and pushed it through, and now at the oncology clinic it's another woman, a little older than me, who prescribed the best chemo ever. It's not only the medication itself but a whole set of painkillers, stomach protectors, and others to avoid negative effects as much as possible. It was on for about 24 hours; I stayed overnight and left when the doctor had explained everything to me in detail about my treatment.

I like the female versions better. I feel I'm not left out of these important questions of my life. My point is not that different people give me different things, because in that case, both would mean something passive from my side. I like to take an active part in my own life; actually, I want to be the screenwriter, the director, and the leading actor in my own movie.

It has not always been like that.

I have to admit, being passive was in a way my choice. After my difficult adolescence with my mother raising us alone, feeling bitter and frustrated all the time, being a single woman didn't really seem to be so much fun. And when I got to know Islam, I was amazed by the status of women it offers. She is literally a queen, carried on the throne all through her life. A whole set of regulations regarding her rights guarantee that she will never have to worry about her rights being granted. So since I was not coming from a family that would guarantee such a situation, I thought that by getting married to *a religious person whom the whole community approved*, I would be just like a queen as well, as I have read in the books.

I wanted my rights back. I wanted the circumstances that would guarantee they would always be met. It seemed to be fair. And it was.

What wasn't fair – and I'm still surprised, reading the Quran every day where everything is crystal clear – was that people today simply don't follow it. They don't act upon responsibility and accountability; they do anything they can to get away with it. They seem to have forgotten that God knows their intentions and sees their hearts. And I'm not only talking about everyday people, but learned scholars too. If something can be twisted and turned into something explainable, their job is done. There is no search for justice; people looking away from missing rights and *sure she didn't want that*. If a woman is not fighting for her rights, it means that she agrees that she won't get any of them. But if she is fighting, she is difficult and she should be patient.

God-given rights are not given by people who represent the right things according to God.

So my dream of being carried on a throne got destroyed among the banana boxes where my clothes are stored (again), and then in the hospital bed where I ended up after a year-long struggle for my independence from a marriage where my rights were gradually taken – all of them.

So no more passivity.

No more power to unjust patriarchal systems.

I will take the steering wheel of my life and drive it to a place of care, understanding, and support. To a life of responsibility and planning. To learn, to experience, to be honest, to work, to help, to love, to create, to restore, and to be happy.

And I'm not going to stop with my life.

What I want is to provide a support system for women still struggling within the psychological spider web of oppression where they are gaslighted into believing that by leaving, they are doing something wrong.

It's extremely dangerous as that's the way patriarchy continues. Because, before their divorce, my parents also lived in a marriage where my mother would sacrifice her own life for the ideas of my father, I grew up with a notion that this is the way to do it. Passivity breeds passivity, and that's what gives life to patriarchy.

It's time to end it.

The water is shrinking. Marina is getting her mobility back step by step. She loses her hair and eyebrows but is getting back to her shape. She thinks about the water of life, which her holistic doctor talked about. Chemo is indeed that for her. She takes a taxi to the hospital, which is on the hillside, but comes home walking. Mageed is at a nice, friendly school that Marina used to attend. He makes some new friends. Yunus is in love with his grandma, his only stable point for the moment.

How to prepare for divorce?
04.10.21

Haram police, I'm sorry, but well, divorce is halal. It's never really a choice. It's never something you do as something you like. It's never what you planned. It hurts and disrupts lives. But sometimes that's what you need to do. To save those who belong to you, to save your mental health – or even more than that.

The first thing we need to prepare ourselves for is to be strong and firm in our decision. Obviously, it starts with Istikhara. We need to recognise red flags and distinguish naivety from genuine positive expectations. Yes, we wait for the best, but if we have been forsaken multiple times; we need to look into the possibility that a certain behaviour is not the result of outer factors but is among the characteristics of our significant other.

It's hard to face these issues and it takes a lot of time and consideration. But once we have made our decision, we need to honour it as it is not a joke, it is a serious issue, based on a commitment to our heart, mind, and soul.

The ideal scenario is that we go to ask for counselling when there's still hope. Unfortunately, it often doesn't happen as we are conditioned not to ask for help and not to let anyone have a sneak peek into the marriage. If we still manage to ask for advice, it's possible that we get some *there you go, here comes nothing* sort of advice, like *tell your husband to do this and that*, while the whole issue was that you can't make him understand the facts. These events just discourage women from asking for actual advice, so at the end, they will only turn to the authorities when they see no other solution. But that decision is final.

It is very important to make ourselves clear in this matter. We will save a lot of time and effort for ourselves and others if we say clearly from the beginning that no, we don't want reconciliation. We are not here to make it better. We don't see the continuation of marriage as a solution, so any attempt in that direction can be suspended. We need to state it as firmly as we are determined inside. They might try to talk us out of our feelings. They might try to mention everything that could break a woman's determination. They will mention children growing up without their father (not like the time they spent without their father so far was our fault in any way) or the number of years this marriage has been going on (and is still lacking basic feelings of trust and mutual respect). So yes, we still want to go on with the divorce.

We need to be familiar with our rights and the way Islamic courts work. If they have a lawyer, a Qadi, it's easy, as they have the right to dissolve a marriage.

If there's no Qadi, but they perform marriages, they are still entitled to perform divorces, but it could happen in a way by asking the husband to divorce his wife. That might be a problem because he could set up conditions when the whole issue started from him not meeting basic conditions. This situation could change the whole outcome, making the accuser a defendant, and we don't want that. So to avoid this, we need to talk through every possibility with the authorities.

Many women have their husband's friends as their waliy. In this case it is rather controversial. It's good to know that we can choose another waliy anytime. We should just go to our present local masjid or to the one we trust the most and build a confidential partnership with the imam. It is very important to ensure that they will really be on our side during the process, and if they feel they can't do it, we should try to find someone else.

I hope that following these steps will be useful in this difficult situation and it can become easier.

Why is it happening?
01.11.21

When I lost my sister رحمها الله more than 2 and a half years ago, I realised that life is not a fairy tale. This life on earth will never be perfect because she is not here. It is full of trials and tests, never-ending problems when you feel like it doesn't make any sense.

After a few years of continuing troubles, you just get the sensation that this life is only a place of suffering. A grey world where the only ray of light is the time we get to spend with those we love. These are not weeks of holidays in fancy places, just a few minutes we get to talk about something deep. Otherwise it's just a series of challenges that only end with us exiting this world. I have concluded that the nature of this life is in fact suffering.

I have already mentioned that getting closer to myself means finding my friends from long ago. I have met a wonderful sister, a beautiful woman inside and out, who I haven't spoken to for many years. She told her story that brought tears to my eyes. The personal and existential lows, and as a result of her heartbreaks, the sickness that had almost taken her life. There was a point where she was fighting for her life, owning nothing but a few items that fit into a shopping bag.

But she never gave up. She went out in the cold and rain alone, only to pray. She believed she would eventually get something better in every field of her life.

And one day it happened. Step by step God restored her situation in every way. Now she is still fighting but she has everything she has ever dreamed of.

I was crying when she told me all that. The heartbreak, the financial difficulties, and the life-threatening illness – all trials I'm so familiar with, that I have been trying to make sense of, to understand the point or the lesson behind it. And here she is, this lovely lady, who's enthusiasm and positivity I have always admired, telling me that it has an end. It will get better. Suffering is not endless and pointless, and it's not simply the nature of this life. It is a trial, but the point is not only to accept it. It is also about how we react.

God is testing us as to whether we can still trust Him. Yes, we have experienced tragedies, but it's only one side of the coin. The sun is still shining, the flowers are still blooming, the air is still there for us to inhale … God's endless blessings still surround us even while our hearts carry heavy burdens.

Being in this beautiful town I have always felt its striking beauty has to be a sign. It is. I'm going to chemotherapy while the sun is shining through the trees, the sky is blue, and the flowers are blooming. Because the fact that God takes something away shows that He SWT can give it back. We just need to ask Him. We just need to understand the proper outset. We ask and He grants us. We look at Him with trust and positive expectation because He is Able to give us anything. We shouldn't lose our trust and hope in Him.

That is what our trials are about.

They are no pointless sufferance.

They show us the power of God – what He can take away, He can give us back, and even more, even better.

We just need to go out in the rain, alone, even if no one cares about us, only to say that prayer out of the deep conviction that He SWT will help us. He gives back our health, our wealth, and our loved ones. And one day, the positive sequence begins ... Maybe it has already started? If we are grateful, He will give us more.

Ps. Yes. There are heartbreaks that will indeed not be resolved in this life. There are losses that remain as such and we will never fully understand the wisdom behind them. We only know it's a legacy to carry on. I wanted to say something uplifting but I couldn't. We miss you so much my dearest sister. God bless you and your little darlings.

Who am I?
03.11.21

I have moved a lot, changed workplaces and circumstances a lot, and it always meant I had to meet new people, to make new acquaintances, to adapt to new situations.

For me, it always meant having a new persona, a new part of my personality, the outside person whom I created step by step by carefully checking the people and the atmosphere for what will and what will not be accepted. To a certain extent it may be fine; obviously, no one wants to be known as the loud one or the crazy one (not like I have ever been close to these), and it's good to respond to the requirements of the environment. But my main focus was on them, and this *persona* did not start from who I am. And to be honest, it was basically not different from the *good girl at school* who's main issue is not to be too visible – except at the few special places where they knew who I was before I knew it.

The fact is, sad as it is, that before I became a 43-year-old divorcee in an economically unstable situation fighting with cancer, I really didn't know who I was.

Maybe this situation where everything is unsure, nothing is taken for granted, and I need to fight for who I am emotionally, physically, and mentally, triggered the deeply buried force, that of my soul, to finally come alive and take control.

As I said earlier, the soul of a person living in any kind of dictatorial system is buried in a cold, wet, mouldy cellar and needs to be freed, cared for, listened to. That's what many people explain as meeting the inner child. But the soul has no age. They were there as babies, children, teenagers, young people, and we do need to address their unmet needs at all these ages, but they possess all the strength of an enlightened adult who is a leader of their life. This is the force we need to free, to let it finally take its rightful place as the leader of my life – as me.

This is what my best friends saw when they told me that I was strong. I, thinking from the persona's point of view, didn't know what they were talking about. The persona, the good little girl depending on other people's acceptance, perceived herself as weak. She didn't know about her strength as she didn't know her soul. She put her self-evaluation in the hands of other people.

But she is not me.

She is an example my mother showed me because that's how she was conditioned. But that has nothing to do with her, and even less with me when I'm among my people, so it definitely has nothing to do with my soul.

This good girl image, this imprint of patriarchy, is the part of my personality that I no longer wish to carry. I took off the costume as my divorce was pronounced.

Now I take my precious time to find out who I really am. What do I really want to do? The jobs I have been doing were mostly just to make ends meet. How do I want to spend my time? And who do I want to spend it with?

Questions that my soul knows the answer to. I just need to listen.

The first chemotherapy arrived at the last moment in August. She gets it almost 3 months after her diagnosis because the famous health centre of the Eastern European university town lost 10 doctors in that summer. That's the result of government policy that seemingly raised, but in reality cut, the wages of doctors. Many of them struggle economically so they had to leave the country.

And she was told to sit and wait patiently. The oncologist thought she had 2 more months. She doesn't tell her. Marina goes to the hospital to receive *water of life*. And she dreams about home, future, family, and love. After the first round, she loses her hair but gets her mobility back. Step by step, her hard water belly is also reducing. She loses her eyebrows. And gains more hope. Cancerous cells that had spread around her peritoneum have gradually reduced. Every third week she goes in for a night and talks with some nice ladies. All of them gave their all and forgot about themselves. Just like her.

By November, the tumour that was previously bigger than 20 cm had been reduced to only 9 cm.

Community
22.11.21

I have been feeling that the system failed me. The community failed me. I did everything that was preached and taught, yet my life went from not moving forward to being completely destroyed. I felt it's just not fair. Why are we constantly told to be patient and not warned about how to spot the things we do not and should not be patient about? Why are we advised to give seventy excuses and not told to stop at the seventy-first as that would be self-destruction? Why is it that we are taught that the best way to ask for help is when we still believe in reconciliation, and then being left alone and not given any help? Why do advisors think *solve it yourself* is advice? And in the end, when you try your utmost and are left with no other choice, why is it that the nicest people are surprised at your decision? Why do advisors use blame, responsibility, and feelings to make you doubt your own God-given rights? And in the end, how can they agree with the destruction of those rights for the sake of keeping good relationships?

The system has failed me. I'm not a failure. Many times I think I should have realised things earlier and made steps, but I don't think I would have been successful. Never in my life have I thought this would happen if I followed the protocol and asked for help to have my rights met, and then my right to get out if my other rights are not met.

This community was my home and family. It was my main circle of friends. We were raising children together, going on *holidays* together (meaning organising youth camps). We lived in and for the community. I didn't do it because I wanted something in exchange for it but because I felt that it was right. Just as I thought the many things we studied and taught about rights of the individuals and the members of a family were also a divinely inspired justice system.

Yet, some people don't practise what they preach. When it comes to women's rights, they cowardly back off and put the women themselves into the combat zone – and they even blame them for not sitting around and waiting.

Well, we won't. That's for sure. I'm not miserable because of a failing system. I'm proud of the strength I have found in myself and in my faith – the true faith I have learnt that's not adulterated by complicated explanations just to be of someone's interests.

After six rounds of chemo, the tumour is only 3 cm. Marina is offered two other, new medicines. One blocks the gene that she and Patricia inherited from their paternal grandmother. Well, the first time she was sick, no one in the hospital was interested in it, not even Mahmood's old friend, the leader of the oncology team there. If she had known at that time that she had that gene, Patricia could have checked herself in time ... there is no such thing as *what would have happened*, but people have responsibilities. Marina knows that when she is strong enough, she's going to question them.

The other medicine, another invention, keeps the blood away from the cancer cells. This second one is intravenous, but it's only an hour, then later half an hour. After it, she takes a nice walk. She is getting her strength back slowly. She wakes from a dream that has become a nightmare and understands she still needs to work on her boundaries. Yunus talks; Mageed cuts his hair and loses his baby fat. He becomes a handsome young man at only thirteen.

Crying souls
07.07.22

More and more people I come across – and myself as well to a certain degree – have experienced deep emotional burnout. When you feel that nothing sparks your excitement. When you don't find anything that you really want. When nothing is interesting.

More often than not, in the background of this feeling, you have profound sorrow. An unprocessed trauma, a disappointment in a person, or in the course of life in general like a loss of a loved one.

This disaster impacted your life to the core and has shaken your whole world

You may be questioning the whole outset of your life: what's the point of it then? There's no real answer, at least not an immediate one. As a result, you retreat from life and go into a numb state, sometimes on autopilot, just to survive the day.

You avoid big questions for fear of the void if they remain unanswered. Initially, you perceive the whole world as empty without the object of your loss, but after the first shock, you are still unable to make real connections or find activities you like for a long period of time. Why?

It's a defence mechanism. Your soul is protecting itself from pain. It is doing so by staying away from any type of attachment. Your trauma has taught your soul that it is not safe to love. That when you love, you will suffer. The object of your love will be forcefully taken from you and you remain in the cold without being hugged, without being understood, without being seen.

You couldn't bear another pain like that so you just wait for the day to become night and wait for the night to become day. You numb your feelings unconsciously, on a deep level, away from your reach, and you just exist. It's the safest way possible for your soul, paradoxically, because the safety of the soul is being loved. But since it has become impossible, the soul goes into numb mode to protect itself from another disaster.

What can you do if you find yourself or others in this situation?

First of all, what not to do. Don't force. Don't force yourself to show up, to look all right; don't force others to do anything *they should be doing in normal circumstances*. Yes, they would do everything in normal circumstances, but the circumstances are far from normal, that's the whole point. Remember, it's on the soul level. Forcing doesn't work. It doesn't change the soul. It might change the surface, the actions or the minds of people, but their souls remain in the same place of pain, or even worse, they will feel misunderstood – and rightfully so.

What to do then? What can you do when you see wonderful people just suffer and not see the beauty of the world? Those years go by and they remain where they are. Or what can you do when you find yourself waking up just to wait for the day to go? You beat yourself up for not being productive and not working for yourself but you are just unable to do it.

Remember, it's on the soul level. What souls need? Understanding. Acceptance. Unconditional love. No compulsion to see the sunlight but to sit with them in the darkness.

As humans we should all have a clear understanding of how we work. We are kind of okay with the body, or at least we have access to many of its cures, but when it comes to the soul, we are totally blind. The soul is you. It's the centre of connection with the world around – people, places, activities. Its language is love and intuition. The *gut feeling* is the soul's direct message to the body, without the rationalisation of the mind. The heart is the place of connection with the eternal, the perfect, the divine, the universal. The soul likes imperfections. Cracked walls and faces. Broken pottery and dreams, and lives kintsugied with gold. The mind is the computer, but the soul is the human behind it. The soul possesses a body, a heart, and a mind. Not the other way around.

In the event of a loss, it's the soul that gets hurt. To solve the material issues, to accept the divine decree, and to mentally understand what happened (and what you should be doing right now) are important steps, but they are no substitute for the perception and understanding on the soul level. Yes, there are many people who seem to have moved on with their lives, but do you know what they feel deep inside? Maybe their souls are crying inside and they don't listen. Their souls are let down twice – first, because of the original problem, and second, by themselves not listening to their soul's cry. That's not a real solution any soul-conscious person would want – especially since we know that the bodies of not understood souls will create symptoms and these could lead to further tragedies and, eventually, more suffering.

There is no other solution. Only acceptance. That's how they are now. Accept it. That's how you are now. Accept it. Let go of the idea that people should feel all right, be all right, and be happy all the time. Look around you, why should everyone be happy all the time? Life is extremely difficult; there are countless wounds people are carrying, and they are hurt day by day. Death, disappointment, financial insecurity, loneliness, injustice, illness, physical pain, humiliation, lies, betrayal, etc. This is what you go through. No need to keep smiling, to make everyone believe, including yourself, that everything is all right. It's not.

But don't think for a moment that I'm promoting negativity. Not at all. What I'm talking about is to listen to your soul's cry. To accept it and not to silence it. To understand it. Sit down with that dear soul, whether it's your own or of someone you love; sit down with them, hold their hands if it feels comfortable, and tell them they are safe with you. You accept them even at this stage. They don't have to keep smiling with you. They don't have to pretend. It's all right. The situation might not be, but their reaction is perfectly fine. Even if it lasts months or years or sometimes even decades. Souls are timeless, they are eternal. They take their time to process pain – and the longer we choose not to listen, the longer they take to get over their pain. Will they ever? Do they have to?

Sometimes souls hold on to their pain because that's something that connects them with their lost loved ones. Just tell them the good news: they will never get over it. A beautiful illustration I have come across showed pain as a huge circle inside another circle that represents life.

Sometime later, the pain circle is still the same size, but the life around gets bigger, and there are other things in it too. That's what happens. Gradually. Step by step.

Pain remains, but it won't cut your fingers every time you touch it, as broken pottery. As with cicatrisation, the wound healing of the soul begins, and the painful edges become the golden glue that keeps you together, shining beautifully and more precious than ever.

The healing of the soul is a natural process. It's how souls are created. You just need to be aware of it, accept it, and understand it. Actual steps, ways, and methods I have yet to learn. But give it time and acceptance. That's how healing begins.

**Loss and love
02.08.22**

One week, the doctor said
The little boy played on the street with the kids
Blissfully unaware of the sentence
His mother got
The clouds on the sky of the village
Turned pink in the sweet afternoon air
Roses continued rambling
And people going to buy food
As they were doing every day
A week before
Just like a week later
The day the little boy's mother will see the sun appear red
Among the pines
For the last time
The village will still be beautiful
Idyllic as the tourists say
But his life will be empty
I remember walking down Kungsgatan
Seeing the shops, indiska was still there, and cafes
And I thought what's the point?
Why do these places exist
If I can't go there with my sister?
How can the sun light the horizon
Among the birch trees
Spreading a soft, sweet yellow colour
If four girls

Lost their mother?
It was more than 3 years ago
What a rollercoaster my life has been
Since I know it's only me who knows
Who I am
Maybe we need to lose our loved ones
To be reminded of who we are?

Marina is flying again. Back to the UK; this time in Kent, to his brother David. When the airport bus goes through Central London, next to Hyde Park, she sheds tears of gratitude. She never dared to hope for it, but God gave it back to her.

After 20 years
07.09.22

Children give us the clearest examples of our deep, primary feelings we might have learnt to suppress long ago.

My three year old is in the stage of limitless imagination. While it makes him feel wonderful getting on aeroplanes in the living room, making his cars his friends, and even taking a ride on the Ninky Nonk, he can easily find himself disappointed when we don't have a key to the neighbour's house or there's no more apple juice, even though he said so.

And that's the hardest. Not only for them. To accept the not very pleasant reality yet to keep on dreaming and waiting for the best to come. To think within this strange time concept. To understand development and change. To be strong enough to face the current situation yet never to lose the label *temporarily*, and at the same time to keep our vision and to do our utmost to make it true. To understand time, something so alien to our eternal soul, and not to let ourselves be discouraged by the painful things we have faced and think *now we are doomed* but to have the guts to stand up and not to give up until we get what we need. To have our trust in the Greater Plan, bigger than our disappointment in what this point of time can give.

The hardest thing to grasp is the difference between *right now* and *eventually*. We need to face the present situation as it is. We shouldn't gaslight ourselves into believing that everything is pink and shiny, but we have to be strong enough to face the truth. The lesson of my past little more than a decade was about that. Yes, what we focus on grows, but that doesn't mean that we can just swipe reality under the carpet. Healing doesn't come from ignoring sickness and calling the hospital *a mountain resort*. Sickness, loss of fruits, wealth, and lives have their very important roles in our lives. They are messages we have to read, understand, and act upon. If we fail to do so and as long as we keep hiding the unopened envelopes, we keep receiving them, perhaps in a much stronger edition.

So what is the message?

OK, let's be brave, let's face the clear facts. We are being taken advantage of, getting rid of our basic needs, and we lose people in different ways, our loved ones or ourselves get devoured by serious illnesses; we are left behind, and don't get what we hoped for. Just a few things that happened to me and my closest circle in the past few years.

The most obvious way to interpret these messages is: *para nosotros, nada*. For us, there's nothing. Life is a meaningless heap of tragedies, a valley of sorrows; all the happiness and joy belong to the afterlife, and we should just work tirelessly towards that, focusing on our duties. Anyway, others have it even worse; we still live in peace and have food on the table so no more whining, let's get our sh't together and keep struggling.

Really? Is that it? That the whole meaning of all the trouble is that *it's the nature of this world*? That it's not paradise so what did we expect?

Should we just keep doing whatever we have done so far? Is there a reason why we keep getting these messages that life on earth is not heaven? Isn't there another message hiding somewhere?

I'm now preparing to drive on the other side of the road and I'm training myself to notice the signals at unusual places. Everything around us are signs. And what are signs for? They inform us about things happening around us as well as our positions. We need to acknowledge them and act upon them. And more often than not, we need to change what we do in response to signs. There are actually very few cases where we should just keep going straight and not even change our speed.

Almost half of my life I have been researching and following teachings that talk about how everything in the world is under the control of the Creator, and how this fills everything with peace and security. The people who gave me the greatest impression during this time were either closely following the rules or were less eager to do so, were active in the community or focusing on their private lives; they came from every different walk of life, but they all shared one common feature: a deep serenity nurtured by their unshakeable knowledge of God and that He is loving of His creatures. Whenever something negative comes, eventually it will be good, or something better will follow. The authentic teachings confirmed that, talking about the Features of God and how He Is as He Was beforehand, He gives His unmeasured blessings to the created world.

Studying theological principles and timeless guidelines is supposed to make us understand why these people think that way and help us practise how they do it. If we understand the theories behind the serenity we see, it becomes easier for us to reach that level, right?

Well, it should happen that way. What I experienced was that the focus of teachings shifted into dos and don'ts; the Compassionate, Merciful, and Loving Creator was portrayed as some kind of a Santa Claus (AstaghfiruLlah – may God forgive us) having a nice and a naughty list, the individual believer consequently becoming more of an anxious checklist filler (I remember we did have those photocopied checklists) than someone having serenity in their soul and mind. And I haven't yet started talking about the effects of all these on the community.

The result is the complete opposite of what I was looking for. I have always thought it was because of our Eastern European culture; decades (centuries) of suppression cannot be erased by two words. But I had to face the fact that people coming from other cultures (suppressed as well, only in different ways) are just as deeply involved in it, if not more so, interpreting the teachings of peace and kindness as stern rules according to the rough mountain lifestyle of their ancestors.

So how can we summarise the process? We face problems.

We either don't believe our own eyes and keep dreaming, or face it and fall into despair.

If I look around and don't find what I want, it doesn't mean that it's wrong and I need to give up dreaming about it. It only means that it will happen later.

Everything our soul contains is created for a reason.

Fears of naughty lists, and the anxiety of ticking checklists and other very smart lists, won't help us find the balance.

Fear of not being enough is crippling the soul.

We need to listen to our souls and go back to the original truths the soul recognises.

So I'm taking a step back. No, not from peace, harmony with, and trust in the Creator and Sustainer of the universe. Not from everything these teachings really are about. But from acceptance translated as self-denial. From the interpretation of the word *surrender* as something done out of fear, with an internal conviction that my needs are unimportant and whatever is going to happen, it will be something I dislike, but I have to accept it anyway. Not as an action done out of trust that I will be taken care of by the One Who controls everything. From the concept of *fighting against our souls*, not from making an effort to do what is beneficial for it and leaving everything that's not.

I'm interpreting the teachings through the filter of my own soul, not leaving it out of the equation.

And that's where I finally find real inner peace. The peace of mind, heart, and soul I saw on many nice people coming from sunny places. The peaceful acceptance out of trust that the One Who creates, heals, and makes has planned a life that might be different from the one we imagined at a certain point of time, but will be much better than it, and it will be according to what our souls contain – as that is also created by the same Creator (by who else?).

This is the kind of *Islam* I believe in. Not the haram police and the fight against ourselves. I'm never going to let my soul out of anything. And my soul recognises its Creator.

Marina arrived closer to her dream place. It's not a walk in the park though. She is back in Eastern Europe for her treatment every third week, with Yunus of course, and in the remaining 2 to 2 and a half weeks, she gets nursery, school, GP registration, the library, feeding the ducks on the pier, the council, benefits, and a health assessment done. Step by step. She starts an access course, enjoys creative writing, the expression of her soul, and for the first time in her life, she even enjoys maths.

The Pier
03.11.22

There's something about the morning hours
If I catch the early sunlight
It makes the place more mine
The breeze gets through my coat
The water has an unexplainable colour
My first companions on the pier
Are the seagulls
Then a stranger is greeting me
Just a minute ago she was here, where has she gone?
Clouds go and come
Dark and light
Grey and salmon
And I'm sitting here with my reflections

Hope, trust, and love
12.11.22

You have a dream
And do your best to achieve it
You work
You pray
To the Creator of the universe
You focus on what you want
You give all it takes
And even more
You work
And pray
Tirelessly
And then life happens the way it does
And you lose hope
You feel lost
Betrayed
And you know this feeling
All too well
This world is an unjust place
It's not what it's supposed to be
Everything is hostile around you
And you can't do anything about it
You are a victim
Determined to suffer
No one can help you
And no one will
They don't care anyway

Everyone else seems to have it all together
Even if they face problems
But they have access to help you don't
Your fate is written
It's not what you wanted
And you just sit passively
Not being able to do
Anything about it
The scenario is set
You are the victim
And they are the oppressors
Whoever they are
Parents, spouses, secret sweethearts
Children, neighbours, shop assistants
Bosses, colleagues, receptionists
People from the community
Teachers, parents from school or nursery
Acquaintances, strangers, office clerks
Your life depends on keeping them happy
But they will never be happy with you
They are angry with you
There's nothing you can do about it
Has it resonated?
What's that deep dark feeling inside?
Where's it coming from?
Is it the way you grew up?
Your parents? Or your parents' parents?
Or some old ancestors from centuries ago
Who was only satisfied with the best
Where there was no room to be happy?
To be honest
To enjoy life

Only for duties
And they were always deemed
Less than perfect
Where is it from?
Maybe all the pain of the last centuries
Added together?
All the oppression your every ancestor
Ever had to face
It is manifested
In this destructive voice
That's telling you
You are not good
Not enough
The only way you can be accepted
Is that you serve others
Never think of yourself
Your needs
You are not here for that
Your only reason is to be useful
Is it because of your background?
Your community?
Your gender?
Darling
Whatever it is
Wherever it is coming from
It doesn't really matter
If you see all the negativity
Your ancestors suffered
The last century
Are you surprised?
When have you experienced kindness?
Acceptance?

Unconditional love?
Don't tell me ... I know ...
Love is the default way of humanity
Anything less than that is harmful
Resentment is dangerous to health
Oppression destroys communities
And self-esteem of the individual
Hate kills
Only love can save you
Love yourself like your life depends on it
It does
Never allow any thought towards yourself
Or others
Especially loved ones
Except love
Cut off everything and everyone
Spreading hate
Just like cancer cells are cut out
Love yourself
Love and trust your Creator
Who only allowed you to
Experience pain
To grow
And to choose love
By yourself
Actively
Because passivity is also a lie
We are here to act on love
And finally
Love others
All while loving yourself
And never allowing anyone

To use you
That's not love or patience
Love doesn't hurt
Patience doesn't tolerate abuse
So if someone can't be loved by you
Just leave them alone
And now just relax
And love yourself

02.12.22

Marina experiences mercy step by step. She gets an appointment at the hospital so she doesn't need to travel back and forth to Hungary every third week. She also gets benefits as someone not able to work. She takes Yunus to nursery and supports Mageed as he is struggling with the new school. And she goes to her creative writing class and learns to express herself freely. On her last trip she went through the Blackwall Tunnel, and as the bus was going through the crooks and turns, more and more light got in the tunnel. She felt it was a metaphor about her life. It's still dark, lots of things need to happen before it gets smooth, but she is gradually getting there.

My words
Were my go-to means
I used to use
To process
Whatever overflows
If I couldn't
Talk about it
Act upon it
Live it
I just sat down
And wrote it
But what if
My words
Could be so much more
What if
They could take the lead
And make me live through them
What if
I could have
Many more lives
Than what could be fit
In this lifetime
In this timeframe
In my circumstances
What if
I could make
All my dreams come true
Through my words

Being a victim
10.12.22

I wanted to write three different articles on the topics of hope and trust, duties and boundaries, and instead it became one piece of poetry. During the process of writing, I discovered how intricate the subjects were and how one topic leads to the others.

It is difficult to have hope and trust if someone constantly feels like a victim. Being a victim, we only live in a scenario where everyone and everything around us either hates us, is angry with us, or looks down on us, or any combination of these. Our only concern is to try to please them and avoid the negative consequences that are unclear: something like, 'They will never talk to us anymore,' which in a scenario like this was indeed real, and doesn't even sound like a terrible thing.

I don't know where this is coming from. It might be some kind of a transgenerational heritage as I have only seen people in the family following it, but in the same way suffering from it and never enjoying it – if not for seconds when they got to be the dictator for the moment.

Feeling like a victim is many things. From being angry with whoever and whatever you come across (yes, even with the kitchen towel you can't find the hook of) to constant negative self-talk and resentment. It seems most likely to be a learnt way – to have copied someone who has criticised themselves all the time. We always say that we should be careful with the way we talk to our children because it will become their inner voice, and it is definitely so. But it seems like the way we talk to ourselves influences them in bigger proportions than previously thought.

I have learnt a negative attitude towards myself. I have learnt it from generations and generations from one side of my ancestors.

Whenever I feel like a victim and I feel that people/situations/anything is against me, I project this inner voice to the outside world.

This is not sustainable. I must be on my own side.

I have always felt something like this, like I had a distorted image of the outside world due to my *black lenses*, but I used it to give a free pass for anyone abusive. I said, 'I can't really understand why people make me feel like that, surely they didn't mean it, I have problems anyway, so let them do whatever they do.' I didn't stand up for myself; I didn't protect myself because I thought it was only my negativity that made me feel bad.

It wasn't sustainable.

Now I don't only know about *having some kind of emotional issue*, I'm also not afraid to look inside it and deal with it. Yes, I didn't love myself. Yes, I projected my lack of love and support for myself to the outside world and have always felt in need. But it doesn't mean that I have to accept and tolerate not being loved and supported by the ones that claim to be standing by me.

I'm checking every small feeling and thought. Whenever there's a hint of a victim attitude, I stand back and stop. My children love me. The office is doing their job. (Actually, it's easier to work on it without negative, passive–aggressive cashiers, shop assistants, ticket controllers, and people on the street who look into your eyes with disgust.)

So I stop and get back to loving myself.

If I don't love myself, I feel like others don't love me. But if I do, I don't feel they hate me or are angry with me.

And only if I love myself can I spot if something is wrong, if someone is really negative towards me. Otherwise, it would only be a basic starting point – that's how the world is, there's no love.

There is.

Our universe is made of love of the Creator towards us. Every atom in nature, including ourselves, is the reflection of this love.

Not to love doesn't make sense – and it's not sustainable. I need to love myself to stay alive.

Tea first
14.01.23

Last time we talked about feeling like victims quite a lot but we didn't talk about the reasons behind it.

Discovering the secrets of our soul is like walking in a forest. What seems to be a darker spot, as we get closer, we understand it's a pine tree, and standing in front of it, we can even see each one of its tiny leaves. The process of understanding is similar, it comes in layers.

The victim mentality is an underlying feeling regardless of how people behave, but certain actions can trigger it, pushing the person into a major PTSD trip. The main question here is not what they said, as, in life, people behave in any way they feel at that moment and we can't ask them to tiptoe around our fears the same way as we wouldn't want to walk on eggshells for anyone. What can we do when we feel like we need to stop existing or to exist simply to ensure others' needs are met?

I entered the usual role, but I had to face the fact that it's no longer possible. I can't just choose to stop existing – I'm fighting for my life. And I can't live in a service mode – that's what's giving me all the resentment feelings. And then I had a very uplifting and eye-opening sensation. I can choose to answer in a different way. I can say I won't just go over to the dying holes and die. I can say that I'm here, imperfectly and unapologetically me, and I might not be able to do everything as expected, but I have to stop hating myself for that.

I learnt to anticipate people's moods and to act accordingly. I learnt that my feelings mattered only … basically, that they didn't matter. If I didn't like something and I expressed that, it was just an uncomfortable situation and the sooner I finished the *circus*, the better it was. I learnt that I was *good* if I was quiet and didn't cause problems. (Rhymes well with people coming home wanting to relax and my existence only serves to provide that.)

I didn't grow up in an abusive home. My parents are intellectuals, they read a lot, about psychology, even about child psychology, and were both committed to continuing only the good they experienced in their respective families and to stop the rest. But it happened in the late 70s and 80s in Eastern Europe and no one is free from the culture they were born into.

I have this learnt voice I was talking to myself in that wasn't loving, wasn't kind. It was reprimanding, questioning, blaming, angry, demanding. That's the way I learnt how to talk to myself.

Facing the hurt I have experienced is not a criticism of anyone; on the contrary, it's a necessary step towards healing and a first step towards the total acknowledgement of my own personal responsibility.

I can spend years or decades blaming people who have influenced my life for a shorter or longer period, but if I don't change this voice in which I'm talking to myself, nothing will change. I'm the one who let myself down and I'm the only person who can change this.

What I have to do is to change the way I'm treating myself, the way I'm talking to myself. I need to stop being angry and demanding and blaming everything I have ever felt on the way people behave with me, and instead,

I should start being kind, loving, considerate, respectful, and all such things to myself as I want to be with others.

This is the only way I can stop the *negative committee in my head*, the victim feeling.

Then came the practical advice of my best friend to drink my tea and put cream on my face before I do anything else. Sounds like a small thing but it's a great help. I need to learn how to take care of myself, after having learnt to listen to my soul.

I have been practising the past few days. Seems to be working.

Even the seagulls
21.01.23

We brought some biscuits for the birds at the pier, and gave them to them in the freezing cold with icy winds. We didn't stay more than five minutes because of the weather and also we were going to be late from nursery.

When we left, I felt that the seagulls (!) would be thinking (!!) why we had come if we only brought a little food and we left so early anyway.

Yes. This is the voice in my head. This is the way I'm talking to myself. This is how I feel about every single person I talk to, every situation I find myself in.

That I'm not enough. What I do is not sufficient so I shouldn't even be here. My right to exist depends on how useful I can be to others – if I can't be, I should not even be here. Wow!

I wonder why I'm talking to myself like that. Where is it coming from? Not to blame anyone, and it's not even necessary if I can get rid of it without knowing the exact origin, I really don't care. But I think it would be useful to know who or what made anyone in my family think or feel about themselves that way. To tell them, to shout it into their imaginary ugly face that 'NO! I am here to live my life! Everyone is here of their own right! No one exists to be a slave or a martyr!'Everyone needs to learn the basic skills of how to support and sustain themselves – not only financially but also energetically, psychologically, and emotionally.

This is what a family should be about: a place where you can learn important life skills safely and not the place where unprocessed traumas are passed through the next generation, replaying the same roles of oppressors and the oppressed.

I'm out.

I'm not here to serve. I'm here because my Creator put me on the earth out of love. My aim is to spread this love – first to myself, as that's the only way to live. And only if I love myself can I love others – and not have fears and resentments towards them.

Those feelings that separate me from the rest of the world are the actual way I was looking at myself. It is filtered through my heart and I perceive it to be coming from others – yes, even from the seagulls.

It would be nice to know the origins of this all, but the most important thing is to put an end to it. I don't know how it started but it will end with me, by me.

I will live my life from now on focused on loving and caring for myself. That's the only way I can survive.

The myth of a saviour
28.01.23

There was this idea I used to like that if women want men to behave like knights, they should behave like princesses and sit and wait in their room in the attic.

Apart from the obvious nonsense of this sentence, and I don't want to take the discourse into the field of sociology, I have found some interesting points.

I remember a story about a queen, maybe Marie or Isabelle (according to my mum's update), who lived in a beautiful castle in the south of France sometime in the Middle Ages. Her husband, the king, probably some Louis, went out to *free the Holy Land* from its inhabitants. He was not the first, and not the last to do so. Anyway, Isabelle was a devout wife and she loved Louis so much that she vowed that she wouldn't take a bath or change her clothes until he came back. He had been staying for 14 years when she finally died. She was quite strong by the way, to survive that long. Obviously, in the Middle Ages the people of Europe had strange ideas about hygiene, but this is extreme even in those circumstances, otherwise it wouldn't have remained as an example of marital dedication.

She indeed was the ideal example of a woman sitting in the dark and waiting for her knight to save her. From her own inability.

Isabelle was just sitting in her room, praying for Louis, thinking about him, writing letters and poems to him. Obviously, as a queen, she didn't have to do anything, nannies raised her children, servants ran the house, politicians and army men ran the country. But, again, as a queen, she had many opportunities. If it was me, and I was sitting in a palace alone with my children in the south of France, I would definitely take them to the seaside and to the medieval towns to some nice restaurants, or I don't know what other opportunities were available at that time. Whatever it was, it might seem dull or strange to us but that was the norm for them. And again, we are talking about the south of France where the sunshine has the colour of the corals and the shadows, the colour of the lavender ... All that seemed grey to her because she only saw Louis in front of her eyes. And that made her lose her interest in life. Her soul was buried under the grief and her life energies were crippled. She was waiting for him to come back and save her from this miserable state. She was just lying down, helpless. Like a baby.

So many people share that as a first experience in this world. Being there, cold, hungry, in pain, and no one comes. Yet the thought of giving up on those who are there to help is impossible. They are the only lifeline.

Later, the deep thought of *I deserve to be treated this way, they can't be bad so I must be* would develop as an explanation of the situation, but the very first sensation is only a feeling of passive helplessness of waiting to be saved.

Action feels like severing that bond that is a lifeline. It is unnecessary, they are surely coming to save us. That's how the passive waiting, a state similar to death, is presented as the only way to live.

Isabelle died in her filthy clothes in her self-made prison at a paradise-like seaside. So many women bury themselves alive, passively surviving but not living, waiting to be saved. To go out and fight for their dreams feels like giving up on the *magic* to happen. They do everything they have to but nothing that would make their souls dance. Why? Over the obvious mind explanations that, 'I don't have time,' there's a deep hope that one day something magical would happen and they just have to wait.

'Just be patient and everything will be fine.' Familiar, isn't it? For years and decades, inner and outer advisors have kept women (and many men too) in the false hopes of staying motionless and then something will change miraculously.

We are not babies.

Most of us are women who have given birth already. The best advice I have ever got about giving birth was, 'It's you who is doing it.' It's not just happening to you, you are not just going through it. You are doing it. You do the pushing, the breathing, the holding breath, you concentrate, you take all your power.

In order for something to happen, it must be something miraculous, because again, those of us who have had babies or are close to babies (I felt it the first time when my first niece was born, so you don't need to be a parent to experience it) know that it is one of the greatest miracles of life, we need to be proactive. We need to gather all of our forces together and push until something new comes to life.

Action is not the opposite of life, it is the very thing that participates in its creation. This is how a miracle happens, not by sitting around passively, because by being proactive, we don't deny our trust in the miracle. We deny our outdated passive role.

To be active, one needs to trust. Much more than by passively waiting while in doubt every other minute. If I'm active, I use my resources in a certain direction. I take risks. I don't take risks if I'm not 100 percent sure that it's going to work.

We are not babies. We are adults and creators of our destiny. We do believe in miracles and trust God. That's why we are not afraid to take risks. We go and do it.

And by looking for the original ways, we must not stop somewhere in the Middle Ages. As my father said at the first interview he gave, 'We must go back to Adam and Eve, well, not exactly, but to the seventies.'

Now we must go back, not to the Middle Ages where women were expected to sit and wait, but to Mary, peace be upon her, who was told right after giving birth to shake a date tree. She did – or at least tried; if you have ever seen a palm tree, you will know that a woman who has just given birth will never be able to shake it – but the reward of her efforts was fresh dates for her and her baby, peace be upon him.

Or let's go back some more centuries, to Hagar. She had to run between the hills seven times looking for water. And then the water came from where she needed it the most, next to baby Ismail, peace be upon him. And we still can drink from that water. I drank from it when I had a tumour the size of a baby and now my ovary is back to its normal size.

That's how important actions are. That's how much they mean trust and belief. And that's when miracles happen.

Reflection on the (Eastern) European woman & (Middle) Eastern man topic 18.02.23

Why is it really that we know more tragedies than success stories? As an aspiring psychologist, even if we are talking about tendencies, I always want to go back to the source of the problem, and even in the case at hand, we do have a common root cause.

The first question we need to ask is whether the woman has converted into the religion of the man, and if she did, when it happened. Based on the old joke that starts 'Comrades, we are in big sh*t! The Germans have attacked us!' we can say, if she hasn't, there's no problem. If she has, the question is, when. If she is in her 30s or later, there's no problem. If in her early 20s or even earlier, well, comrades, we are in big sh*t.

Why am I saying that? I'm a Muslim since my early twenties and I have always thought it would help me in case I were to face marital problems as we would have common ground. If any of us is wrong, we just need to get back to the teachings of the religion, and we would live happily forever together. The only problem is that not everyone takes these teachings as the moral backbone of their lives (without a backbone it can become especially hard). Most of the people coming from some cultures already have a moral support, their own culture. Religion is definitely a part of it so it can provide familiar ground to converts looking for a home in this world, but the base of the structure is the customs and habits of their own (sometimes tribal) society. It has many common points with the teachings of the religion, many of which can be acceptable in certain circumstances (not here), and it also has points that are totally against it, but since it is so widespread, it is commonly accepted. And then comes the personal/societal behaviour of whether someone follows their inner moral consciousness or only the letter of the law.

And why did I say the age of the person accepting the religion counts? Because if an adult person makes such a decision, it will be a logical, rational choice of someone who knows who they are. They know what's right and wrong, they can defend themselves, and they won't get into situations where they will be used and abused, or if they do, they recognise it earlier and get out. They don't understand why smart, precious women who possess a great amount of knowledge about their rights choose and stick in situations where these rights will clearly never be met.

When someone makes a decision around the age of 20, it is their choice as being an adult. You find clear answers to your search for the Creator, you are allowed to think and ask, there are no ambiguous theological questions that you should just believe and swallow. And on the human level, there is a straightforward moral code and a system that stops people from doing wrong. What could go wrong?

Our softness and lack of boundaries. Our naivety. And – just as dangerous as the predators are – the danger lies within our background too.

At the age of 18, or even 23, most people are not done with the recognition and processing of their childhood traumas. If someone has grown up with emotionally unavailable parents, when they discover that their perfectly chosen spouse is emotionally unavailable, they won't take it as a red flag but as something completely normal as the air they breathe. When someone's parents are nice and supportive people but they have anger issues, yelling will not seem like a big deal, that's how people are and there is no *real* problem, they have a roof above their head and food on the table. If, on the other hand, someone has perfect manners, but right now they are in a little trouble so they can't provide support, we can be sure that only those familiar with the situation will tolerate this. Of course, we can always count on society for a little victim blaming and shaming, saying, 'Have sabr sister,' the weak way of trying to keep the status quo intact, going towards a smaller amount of force. But the real question is, why did they (we) only discover the house was burning when some of us literally didn't have a roof? And I can only answer that it's because we haven't processed and healed from our previous traumas caused by our own society. And I'm not saying that in case we had already done it, these marriages could have been saved. I always thought I was not good enough and if I were, everything would be perfect. No, darling (myself 5–15 years ago). If I knew then what I know now, I would have seen as many red flags as on Red Square on the first of May.

This is the reason women don't see their house burning, the reason they stay for so long. Do they learn in Eastern European society to take care of themselves? To have boundaries that come from their souls? To recognise the voices of their souls? Do they know that they can say no and it doesn't mean that they will be left alone and not loved? Do they have emotional support?

Don't they learn to accept anything in order to be accepted? Don't they learn from nursery school that the best way is to fit in and not to speak up? Don't they learn from the time they were babies that their feelings don't matter, their cry is in vain?

If the answer to just one of these questions is no, then we, the Eastern European society, prepare and sell our children, especially daughters, to be used and abused, and to never recognise their problems let alone stand up for themselves.

I'm 44 and I have learnt all that the hard way. This is *being ready for marriage* when, just like the velveteen rabbit, I'm a bit damaged and I can't guarantee anything in terms of time (well, no one can, but it happened to me two times that, according to the tribal customs, I was considered not worthy of any effort).

I wish people didn't have to go through similar ordeals. I wish people looking for God and a just society weren't brainwashed into accepting a situation that goes against the very same teachings. I wish they could find their souls somewhere in the cellar and have the courage to free them.

And I wish they did it in time.

So is it a good idea to marry a Middle Eastern? If you have your soul freed, if you have your boundaries coming from your soul, you will want to connect on a soul level with someone who has gone down their own road. And you will see the red flags coming from anywhere. I don't think the question is whether or not the candidate is Middle Eastern. The real question is, are you an Eastern European?

Let's become phoenixes instead.

Hajering, Maryaming, and the first breeze of spring
15.03.23

I have been doing a lot of "Hajering" lately. First, before we moved in, literally, running between the two hills, and now, trying everything, moving every stone, searching for every opportunity to find food for my babies.

Hajer is often mentioned in a rather derogatory way, perhaps in the case of converts due to the cultural heritage of viewing her role, her status, etc., and in the case of any Muslim – and actually people of any other religion/worldview – due to the fact that a woman who is left alone with her child because of any reason is still looked down upon, provoking sorrow from the goodhearted and anger from those lacking it.

The story of Hajer being left alone with her child in the desert incites many different emotions in people today, when raising children alone for any reason or being a single mother is not considered a rare event. However, mentioning this story, more often than not we see Prophet Abraham (peace be upon him) criticised and her viewed as a poor victim rather than a hero.

Hajer was a hero, a brave immigrant and a founder mother of a nation and a culture. Regardless of the reason why her husband left her there (yes, husband, and the real reason is that it was God's commandment, Him knowing the outcome, not that Abraham was afraid of his first wife), what she did made her a real role model for women of today.

We, women of the 21st century, have different ideals than our counterparts from the preceding centuries. A woman today is expected to stay strong in any circumstances, be brave when something new comes up, and grab any opportunity that could be beneficial for her and her family.

That's exactly what Hajer did. She ran between the hills tirelessly until the angel appeared right where her child was. She made an actual well for the water to flow in a regulated way and not uncontrollably around the land. And when people arrived, she shared the blessing of the water with them as living in a community would be beneficial for her and her child as well.

Our religion honoured her efforts by making it part of the Hajj rituals. Yet Muslims in the 21st century still tell women to sit around and be quiet, not to be proactive but to wait for someone to save them, and never, in any circumstances, should they talk to unknown men – aib, haraam! If Hajer lived according to these expectations, we wouldn't have Zamzam, as the blessing came while she was running up and down as a recognition of her efforts, we wouldn't have Mecca, as the tribe came due to seeing the birds circling around the water, and very simply, we wouldn't have the Arabs.

Hajer and Ismail would have most probably died of thirst in the desert. That's the result of sitting and waiting patiently, as they require.

I did that for 10 years. I'm never going to do that anymore. What I do now is to run between the hills – and these here are quite steep ones – looking for sustenance, blessing, life, solutions for myself and my children.

Hajer can be a role model for single mothers too, even if she wasn't actually one because the reason why she was alone is judged only by God. Only He knows all the reasons why someone is *justifiably absent*, unjustifiably absent, or it was very simply her personal decision based on her reasons. We have no right to ask or to form an opinion on someone's life choices and the reasons behind them we know absolutely nothing of.

A woman in the Central Mosque almost spat on me when after 3 minutes of conversation she told me to have another child (???) and when I didn't want to get into the details of my health; I only mentioned the other inhibiting fact, that I was divorced. How dare I be divorced? Me, a convert who should be grateful to be allowed into their precious community. She had no idea of my life, of my reasons, and actually there could be much worse reasons, as happen to many people, for example, violence. She didn't know, I could have been running from being beaten up. All she knew was that I was divorced and this sole information provoked an anger in her towards someone she didn't know anything about.

And these people call themselves those who live in peace and harmony accepting the will of God.

What they accept is a centuries old cultural norm of women being submitted, not to God (as Hajer did) but to men who decided about their lives and death. Women should just stay quiet, sit around and wait, or practically do everything at home, not to have a moment to think about themselves, but to serve others. They think that's what women are created for, to serve and not to think.

I think this thought is quite intercultural. We see it in Europe in the Middle Ages and many effects of it were only erased as late as in the 20th century. Doctors as late as the 18th century were discussing whether women have souls or not. Some of this thought is still around, for example, women getting less pay for the same work than men. In fact, when I chose Islam more than 20 years ago, one of the factors of my decision was its view of women's role and their rights. According to Islam, a woman enjoyed more rights in the 6th century than a western woman today. I never expected that the culture of the people following these principles could be so far from it.

Another famous role model, venerated throughout cultures and religions, is the saint Virgin Mary or Maryam. She is mentioned among the most righteous women and is often cited as an example of piety. A story in the Quran mentions that while Maryam was giving birth, a spring gushed forth under her so she could wash herself, and another miraculous event, that she was told to shake a palm tree and fresh dates would fall down so she could gain energy.

If you have ever given birth, you know how impossible it is. You are weak, your whole body is in pain. To stand up is hard enough, let alone shaking trees. And if you have ever seen a palm tree, you know that even a strong athlete cannot just shake it so that the fruit falls down. It's not like a branch of grandma's old cherry tree.

Why was she told to do something she just cannot? Was the date falling down a direct consequence of her action? I think it was something like in the case of Hajer, a reward for her effort. And I think she had to do it to feel that she could. God could very simply cause the tree to throw its fruit as He actually did, and as He created the spring from nothing – and so many things, for the record. But Maryam, a single mother, rejected by her community, at the moment when she is most vulnerable and most in need of help from humans – no. She needs to act alone, and she receives the rewards.

God could send down all my sustenance at once, as He SWT did the last time I came here with my babies when the smaller one was not much bigger than a newborn. I did my runarounds, but once we were established, we lived in security until the next chapter of my life arrived. This time is different. Now everything happens gradually. I have to shake every single tree for some dates to fall down. That's enough, just until the next one.

But I don't mind. In fact, I proudly accept this honour and I'm grateful for being able to do it – especially after all I have been through.

And now as I look around, I see beautiful flowers and the sun shines brightly some days, but the air is still cold and the wind is strong. It's still hard to imagine sitting in the park and enjoying a picnic, but I know it will happen one day. This is the weather I was born into. This is my first impression of this world. It's cold but I have great hopes. I believe that the sun will warm the weather one day. I see some beautiful flowers and I know the others are coming soon. I'm cold now. I don't know how it will happen. But I know that it will.

Until then I continue to run between the hills and shake every tree.

From January, Marina's treatment is in the neighbouring town; she receives exactly the same medicines as before. She doesn't need to fly back and forth to Hungary every third week, which has been exhausting in every way. And on 2 February, 4 years after the loss of Patricia, she finds their home. It is a dream come true. The house reminds her of the one she lived in in Walthamstow with her friends Jeannette and Sunny, and it has a beautiful atmosphere. She buys a floral-patterned sofa set and four chairs in the charity shop. Beate comes with her husband and they bring a table, TV, TV stand, shoe rack, and kitchen appliances. Her dear daughters, who were in Marina's group back in the Hungarian Islamic Centre some 14 years ago, now adults, also share the costs of her fridge and washing machine. Marina is overwhelmed by their kindness.

She orders a vinyl floor for the kitchen and it looks wonderful, even the landlord admires it. She buys flower bulbs in the pound shop and plants them with Yunus in the little backyard.

Lemon cottage is what I call you
A simple yellow house for any passer-by
A safe haven for me
In the midst of struggles
A port where my ship
Has finally found refuge
After being torn and twisted
Among thunder and waves
For so long
My calm place
Where I can finally
Just be myself
Where I can breathe
As a shipwreck lying
Under the bright yellow sun

Today
12.04.23

I hoped this day would go unnoticed just like countless others during holidays when you don't know the date. In Ramadan I had even more chances as I was focused more on which day of Ramadan it was, but it didn't happen. The whole day I was aware that it would have been my fifteenth wedding anniversary. And it makes me sad.

'Why?' you could ask me, and even I'm asking myself. It was me who wanted to end it, and my life is much better now thank God. Although I am really grateful for every experience and I know it couldn't have happened in any different way, being rational, leaving the UK for an Eastern European country is never the smartest decision, even if someone marries an actual prince in shining armour. And coming back was very difficult, so I'm just glad it's done. Why am I still sad?

Maybe it's my unheard, unexpressed feelings that gathered throughout the years that I didn't want to face. My situation, respect for the people, the family, the community made me silent about my personal feelings, and it led me to keep them secret from myself too. I wanted to prove it can work so hard that I failed to spot the signs that said early on it didn't. I know now what suppressed pain, sorrow, and bitterness can cause so I'm here to listen to every single pain my soul is telling me.

Generally, in a relationship, even if it ends, there's a period of happiness. When both of them are fully giving themselves to the passion and there's nothing else for them in the whole world. It can happen that it's restricted to a limited time because of some circumstances, but it might just make it even more exciting. There has to be a time, if it's a day, let that be, dedicated only to the couple. That's what anniversaries are for. Or if it's a random event, that's fine as well, but I have never experienced being held up as important or celebrated, not for a day or a half of a year. I don't think that's too much to ask in any situation. In fact it happened that two times I arranged everything for a nice date night and was rejected with some lame excuse that he was tired.

These were the red flags I hadn't noticed, but they became the first nails in the coffin of this marriage. No matter how I tried to explain it away, it made me sad, and the fact I wasn't listening to myself made me feel like I was working against myself.

Actually, all the time in my marriage I felt, in a way, that I didn't want to cause too much trouble, and not to take up too much space.

And then I'm asking myself why something started to take up space inside me.

I'm not here to blame anyone. That's not what this chapter is about. I'm doing my inside work on finding out why it took me so long to realise it didn't work. There were unhealthy patterns I thought were all right, and that I just needed to try and keep trying on and on and it just isn't the way. This chapter is not about that either. What I'm doing now is only listening to the sorrow I had many years ago. I'm telling myself it did matter, my feelings were valid.

Because only after listening to the past, sitting with sorrow humbly, accepting its lessons, can we fly without burdens towards the future.

So now I'm just sitting on my sofa, looking out the window at the green trees and enjoying the sound of rain. Happy self-care day to myself.

15.05.23

New screenings reveal that some of the cancerous cells have started to spread again, so the doctor suggests a review and chemo again. Marina gets scared and blames herself. Yes, she had worried too much the past half year. Yes, immigrating with two children, alone, being ill, is really stressful. Maybe she has really made a mistake … Her friend and fellow fighter, Beate, reassured her that her place is here and everything will be all right.

It is. Marina is referred to the gynaecology department where she talks to a bright and friendly young doctor. She proposes an operation with three potential outcomes: laparoscopy only, the removal of every organ affected by cancer, and the dreaded third, a stoma, permanent or temporary.

Marina would only know once she woke up …

Hope or passive acceptance?
26.06.23

I know they didn't mean to hurt me. But they did.

Spying on people's intentions is not my duty. OK, I should assume the best and I know they really didn't mean it.

Nevertheless, I'm hurt.

It's like this parent thing. You should honour your own feelings regardless of how well meaning the others were.

My feelings have nothing to do with the fact as to whether others are nice people or not.

They can be the nicest people on earth, but if I'm hurt, I have the right to feel that way.

I'm honouring my soul and asking her how the feeling is.

What does it look like?

Degradation.

I, a 45-year-old woman who has hopes of living a full life one day, and to find a love I have never known, was compared to a 90-year-old lady who's happy to be alive. Yes, I'm happy to be alive too, AlhamduliLlah, and I know it's a miracle and I do have a dangerous illness, but I still want something more in life.

Maybe this is the point where my Achilles heel is.

That I felt so many times in my life that wanting more isn't acceptable. That I should just sit down, be quiet, and be happy for having what I have.

When I told my classmates in secondary school that I wanted to go to Italy, a girl (who has since committed suicide) told me that it was not going to work.

This shows that my point is not that I'm angry with the people who tried to stop me. No, I feel sorry for them; they were carrying much heavier baggage – that eventually proved to be too heavy for them to carry.

When they expressed their concern, it wasn't about me, it was about the way they see the world.

Why does it hurt me?

Because I have always missed encouragement.

You can do it!

Go for the best!

These sound strange in the part of the world where I grew up.

My soul, raised by Eastern Europeans, trained to accept whatever life throws at it, can't bear any more passive acceptance.

Beletörődés. That's what they call it. To be broken in order to fit into something you don't.

To accept things you normally don't like and keep smiling about it was considered the right thing, a desirable behaviour, especially for a woman.

Countless of these women suffer from many different types of diseases.

I can't bear a single moment of passive acceptance anymore.

This is what made me sick. I want to heal. I can't heal having the very same mindset that made me sick.

Hoping to heal but only to a certain extent is not really hope; it's passive acceptance in disguise.

I'm not angry with anyone.

But I detest passive acceptance.

Refuse to hope with limits. Hope has no end.

I will heal fully and live a full life in sha Allah. I hope from God – and God's Ability is unlimited.
So is my hope.

The past weeks and months, guests have come and left: her dear friend Mandana, to conclude one of the greatest tasks in her life; her nieces, Patricia's elder daughters Samira and Ysra, who did their first trip alone, and are on their own road finding themselves after the loss of their dear mother; then three other wonderful friends: Beate, Safiyya, and Roxanne; and her mother, Sarah. Beate had gone through a similar path with divorce, immigration, and cancer, and she helped Marina with her positivity and also with practical help when they moved in. Safiyya has also supported her throughout her path; they shared their discoveries about the discrepancies of the community. Roxanne is also on her way to creating a life fully for herself, ditching others' expectations. They had worked together years ago with Marina on the fashion project and now she wants to go further in this direction.

The house is full of love and laughter. Everything is different this time. She can talk to her mum like two grown-ups, without hurt, passive–aggressive remarks, untold resentments. She even tells Marina about her own unborn sister. This explains everything. Sarah was waiting for her sister to be born when she was two. She had two brothers who would only play with each other, and Sarah always felt left out. Then her parents told her about her little sister who was about to be born. But little Stella was never born. Sarah felt sadness from her parents – she knew she could never ask them what happened to Stella. So she just played with her dolls alone; then as soon as she learnt to read, books became her companions. She had always felt an outsider in this world.

Marina understood everything. Without Patricia, she would probably have ended up being the same as her Mum. Patricia has always been the stronger, the smarter, the more beautiful, the more popular … not because she wanted to be, and actually Patricia herself never felt like that, but because she had her unbreakable soul. Marina learnt from her how to deal with people, how to be herself, and since she has gone, Marina considers it her mission to uphold Patricia's legacy.

Sarah wasn't that lucky to have a sister, a best friend, a help to connect the outer world. She remained in her own thoughts, most comfortable among her books, researches, and Latin language handwritten documents. She has become successful in her field; there's nothing to belittle, but the first time she listened to her soul was in her 60s in Italy.

The good news is, Stella exists. She is there, somewhere, in that other realm, sitting with Patricia and her unborn daughter, Amira *baby* – who is about a 14-year-old beautiful girl by now – at some wonderful seaside terrace. To have a cool aunty must have been a relief and a blessing for Patricia. And it is for Marina too. It's almost like having a fairy godmother. And most importantly, it helps her understand her mother more.

And now she needs to go to the hospital.

Her creative writing poetry assignment helped her prepare for it.

Budget

My life is on a budget
I only want to breathe
The cool wind on the summit
The freshly autumn breeze

My body has its budget
How long it lasts, we'll see
I am taking care of it
I want to see the sea

My mind is on a budget
I don't have time for scenes
I'm saving me from crisis
And think about the peace

My soul is on a budget
And what it means to you?
If you're here to screw it
I will show you the door

My heart has its boundaries
It has its own budget
It had to learn the hard way
Don't give before you get

Da questa malattia
Io ci guariro
La mia bella vita
La difendero

Enough

There
Take my hand   *Mia anima dice basta*
Grab a bite
It's just there for you to
Take
What you want   *Mia anima dice basta*
From my life
Isn't it the way you
Live   *Mia anima dice basta*
With someone
That you love   *Mia anima dice basta*
You're just there for them to
Give   *Mia anima dice basta*
All your life   *Mia anima dice basta*
And some more   *Mia anima dice basta*
Even though you can't give   *Mia anima dice basta*
More   *Mia anima dice basta*
Endless fight   *Mia anima dice basta*
'Til one day   *Mia anima dice basta*
Your soul screams
That's enough!

How will I wake up

Come mi svegliero
Dimmi
Come mi svegliero

With deep wounds
Without results
The way it was
Between the woods

Come mi svegliero
Dimmi
Come mi svegliero

With a hole on my body
Losing my dignity
And every hope
To be cloudlessly happy

Come mi svegliero
Dimmi
Come mi svegliero

Or maybe
This minefield can be cleared
And I won't have to fear
What my future brings?

Tell me how I'm going to wake up

Shift of focus

Can I please forget my life
Just for these two weeks?
Can I see the sun to rise
Without all my fears?

Can we talk about the films
Or the politics
Or what Jo's ex-husband did
In two thousand and six?

Can we go to Richmond Park
At dawn to see the deer?
Then we sit in one of those
Floral-themed cafes

Let's get lost in Camden town
Let's buy a Turkish lamp
Can't take it home so I will choose
A kimono instead

Nice bucket list, isn't it?
Get away from real
Problem is it doesn't help
Cope with all my fear

If I did all this and more
I wouldn't forget
My fate is what's waiting for
Me in that white bed

It's my chance to face my life
In its true colours
I won't make it look so nice
Betraying my soul

We can learn from everything
Cancer teaches this:
You're allowed to take up space
You don't have to shrink

What if I grow into my
Lifesize potential
I will not need to be shown
Such an example

If I grow, then nothing needs to
Grow inside of me
If I live, then nothing needs to
Live instead of me

My to-do list is still there
But let's make it a plan
Not something to do before
Rather when I win

La sirena

Come vedo questi anni
La mia strada verso me
Questi passi dopo passi
Una storia dentro se

Revisiting painful chapters
Wouldn't want to change it back
She lost everything that mattered
But she got her real voice back

She's a mermaid back in water
After a lifetime on land
Freeing from the net that caught her
She's learning to sing at last

She is full of wounds and lesions
Freedom didn't come for free
But she's swimming in her ocean
Despite all her injuries

Non avere mai paura
Riprendere cio chi sei
Non e la tua vita vera
Like a fish out of water

Marina is in the hospital. When she woke up after 9 hours of surgery, she asked whoever she met, 'Is it done?'

It is.

And with no stoma. The best possible way.

People are wonderful.

Nurses and doctors come and are genuinely happy about her improvements day by day.

She manages to sit up more and more, washes herself, walks baby steps.

Like she did to her soul …

Everything bad has been cut out of her.

She is cloudlessly happy and grateful.

RHM The solution – the most missing quality of our society
13.08.23

I love Arabic grammar. Most of the words have a three-lettered root that encompasses a pool of possible meanings, all having something in common. From these roots, with the addition of other letters, we can form countless nouns, verbs, or adjectives according to an amazing set rule.

The most familiar could be perhaps salaam that means peace, with the root S-L-M. It is the root of the world Islam as well, which actually means something like a wilful acceptance of the facts (ordained by God) that provides peace of mind. Not submission, not suppression, even more not suppression of creatures. (OK, grammatically, it could mean submission, but psycholinguistically, I would avoid the use of this word in the presence of anyone – including myself – who has grown up in a submissive environment and/or oppressive society.) Knowledge is to be aware of the fact. Wisdom is to know when and how to tell them.

R-H-M is another triconsonantal root of many Arabic words containing a wide range of meanings that includes pity, mercy, compassion, kindness, sympathy, caring, etc. It actually means all the manifestations of unconditional love. According to a strongly referenced prophetic teaching, the *rahma* (= mercy, compassion, kindness, sympathy, caring, etc.) of God is more than 100 times bigger than all the rahma that ever existed on earth over time, including the human and animal world. So how could someone think about God as someone '*not merciful*'?

Another important derivation of the RHM root is rahm, the womb. It shows us a lot of examples of being a mother and how to treat yourself in case you haven't received all the unconditional love and kindness and mercy in childhood. Perhaps it makes so much sense to me now as I don't possess the organ itself anymore, yet I'm trying to embody all the features it actually embodies. I understand from it that as a mother, my main way of existence is providing a safe haven for my children, to accept them unconditionally, to love them as they are, to show kindness to them, to be caring, to feel sympathy for them, and to be merciful with them no matter what.

I have many friends, thank God. Very few of them I talk to daily/weekly, but there are others who, no matter how long time passes, we can talk about the most important things immediately. I can't be grateful enough to one of my dear friends from this latter group who shared her deep struggle with a guilty conscience for not knowing how to draw a line between accepting her child as they are and following her principles (the grown up child apparently goes against them). The whole idea of this chapter actually came from these meaningful conversations with my dear friend.

The way religion was taught to us was partly as a law book and partly as some people's attempt to recreate their society in a land that was already prone to being suppressed. The red oppression was painted green, and the unspeakable fear of the black car stopping in front of the house at dawn (an actual threat our parents' generation lived under as children) has turned into the *pious fear of God* for not completing religious duties and not ticking off enough on our checklist of good deeds. What remains is the fear of an authority that is only interested in deeds and not the thoughts and feelings behind them. How absurd! How many times do we read that God sees our hearts and not what we do outwardly? And there are so many things against the idea that God would actually be like a heartless tyrant. He is Compassionate – and is actually the Possessor of rahma (= mercy, compassion, kindness, sympathy, caring, etc.) for every single creature. He even provides oxygen and sustenance to sinners, so is Merciful. He gives extra to those who love Him – not trying to tick every box on the checklist out of fear. We know that He is Kind, Forgiving, the Seer of our hearts, is closer than our jugular vein, meaning that He understands us better than we understand ourselves, yet we see and portray Him as if He was less compassionate and understanding and loving than a relatively soft hatred human is able to be. What's our excuse? And what's our reason? That we have not been freed from the shackles of tyranny that have surrounded us in the air since we were conceived, were infiltrated in our mothers' milk, and have been everywhere around us ever since, as the poem 'One sentence on tyranny' says. And then came people from another suppressed society and explained so many just legislations – yet in everyday life they follow another suppressive way where only outer actions matter and not the hearts. The only time we notice they possess that organ is when they form a long line in front of the cardiologist on health day.

Why is it so? Why do they present mercy as a set of requirements? Why do we accept submission instead of peaceful tranquillity? And why do we continue this, giving those who have been in our rahm, who yearn and live from our unconditional acceptance, a new set of complexes of inadequateness? How can any sort of principle be more important than the person themselves, their need to be loved?

Why? Because none of us experienced real mercy, compassion, acceptance, unconditional love.

Because those who had been charged with loving us unconditionally had already been broken by the time they had us. And the same happened with those who raised them, and to those who raised them, and on and on and on. There's no documented time of a society built on mercy, acceptance, and unconditional love.

People believe that the enforcement of principles on new generations is the cure as it's the right way, and are surprised when they rebel against our lofty ideals. What we fail to understand is that before any elevated, pious way can be accepted, one needs to feel accepted. One needs to know why. If it's God teaching us something, we need to know God. We need to know He loves us unconditionally and that He is suggesting to us a way of life that is benefiting us. It's not an order. We will not fall out of His mercy if we fail to follow His advice. There's no way to fall out of His mercy.

We, middle-aged people who grew up in oppressive societies, had to learn from the moment we were born that in order to be accepted, one needs to give up our own needs. Babies weren't *allowed* to cry, so they learnt to disregard their own feelings of cold, hot, wet, or hunger in order to please those on whom their lives depended. And then in kindergarten, in school, in the family, in society, in higher education, in the workplace, we met a new set of requirements we needed to meet in order to go on, to live, and no one cared about what we wanted. After a while we didn't care either, we lost all connection to our own gut feeling, to our soul. Why? Because we weren't treated with rahma. We have only known rules to abide by and no unconditional love – we have never received it. So when we were presented with a just system, we admired its justice, but we perceived it as a new set of laws, and not the manifestation of mercy, compassion, kindness, sympathy, caring, and unconditional love. Why? Because we had never experienced it.

How can we say we haven't experienced rahma if we believe that's the main quality of God? Haven't we seen all the wonderful examples of our life when He saved us from calamities, when He answered our prayers, when He opened up doors we thought were closed forever? What's wrong with us?

Nothing. There's nothing wrong with us. We just can't love following orders. It's not how it works. It's not how we work. How we are created. We can perceive love if we experience it directly. If our parents were unable to give it to us due to the same problem, we can give it to ourselves. We can accept ourselves unconditionally. We can be compassionate with ourselves, show ourselves sympathy and kindness. And yes, most probably there will be times when some of the points on the checklist won't be ticked. But it's all right because we are learning to operate from the place of love, not from the place of a desire for adequacy and compliance. Only if we love ourselves unconditionally will we experience the love streaming to us from God.

Only then, if our integrity, or what we believe at the moment to be that, is not swiped off the table, not denied, not judged, but accepted as it is, can we experience real mercy – and consequently, we will be able to follow any sort of guidance or advice. In the situation when our authenticity is not required to be given up in order to have a connection, we can rebel as they are, and we can learn a lot from our children. How?

Because the next generation doesn't operate from fear. And it's partly our merit. When we held them as babies when they cried, when we fed them whenever they were hungry and not *every 3 hours* as was prescribed, when we sat down with them and asked them what's wrong and didn't order them to stop whining, we nurtured their souls. We managed to provide them with part of the rahma we haven't even experienced because we felt that's part of our fitrah, our natural way of being.

Consequently, our children don't believe they need to deny themselves in order to be accepted, and we can take pride in this. We helped them heal from a transgenerational curse and it's wonderful. We have started a road we haven't really understood, just felt that it's better, but we stumble from time to time as we don't really know the next steps. Also, with little babies, rahma comes naturally, but with partly grown teenagers and tweenagers, it can become a question of dominance. They are stronger than us; we raised them that way, but now we might feel they turn against us, denying our principles. And we can't pour from what we don't possess.

The next inevitable step is to channel rahma towards ourselves. To learn to love ourselves unconditionally. To turn to ourselves with sympathy and care. To understand ourselves, to heal our wounds. And by doing it, by going through the process to learn to love ourselves, we will experience the fact that God's love has always been there. It has never left, never changed. That whatever we have gone through was only for us to finally find ourselves.

We need to experience our own unconditional love in order to perceive the love of God that has always been around, and also, in order to be able to love others unconditionally. And no, it's not a requirement again to love everyone like that. But our children are an exception. They are entrusted upon us in order to be loved by us unconditionally. In order for us to convey the love of God to them. And this is the way. Not the restrictions, the rules, and laws, and absolutely not the way of full or partial retraction of unconditional love. That's not how they will understand what's right. Every rule is actually a manifestation of love, but for anyone to accept it fully, by heart, not by force, one needs to know the source of that love and needs to experience it.

Is it too farfetched from piety? From righteousness, from following God's rules?

During the first 13 of his prophethood, Prophet Muhammad, peace be upon him, never introduced a single ruling. No obligations, no prohibitions. Only talks of who God is, how He dealt with previous nations, how we can see His love and mercy throughout the millennia of human history. Only when there was an opportunity to create a society based on justice for everyone were guidelines gradually introduced, and they were called *advice* to the people and their leaders.

Muslims also get offended when they are told. 'Islam was spread by sword', and they love to cite the example of Indonesia where the nice manners of the Yemeni traders were the main reason for the spread of the religion. What we fail to recognise is that withdrawal of love where it is necessary has the same effect as cruel oppression. Not giving unconditional love to our children can kill them. Being strict with them and imposing even the best principles upon them is the same as spreading truth and justice by sword.

We can try other ways, but this is how psychology works. This is how we are created. By our Creator. Out of rahma.

Marina is sitting on her flower-patterned sofa. Fresh fruit and herbal tea are on the coffee table in front of her. Her hair is beautifully wavy; she started to lose some, but it's still fine. Second chemo is next week; she will ask again about the ice cap that Beate has suggested to her.

She is editing her book. It is an overwhelming yet satisfying task. To go through again all the pain of the past 4 years is definitely tough, yet seeing where she came from is really uplifting. Was it really that oppressive, the way those people portrayed *mercy*? That's quite scary. It's so liberating to be over it. To be able to breathe freely, to understand by mind, heart, and soul that God is Merciful. And for that she had to get away from the *religious* people ...

She had to experience mercy first hand instead. She received sustenance, step by step. She received a home. She received proper care. And also her surgery went the best way.

She was given wonderful friends and other people were removed from her life.

And she was shown some first steps towards her ikigai.

She trusts and loves God more than ever before.

Sunny streets with stress in bloom
Where my young years have passed through
Why didn't I understand
The value of this promised land
Didn't know what I now do
What matters is inside you
Other people's acceptance
Doesn't prove your existence

Search your soul through everything
In good and bad, there is blessing
Finding your real guiding light

You won't get lost in the night
Everything will lead you through
If your compass is your soul

APPENDIX

Kintsugi mosaic

Kintsugi is an ancient Japanese way of restoration. Broken ceramics are not thrown, but all their pieces are collected and placed together as they were, but not to make it seem intact. The break is emphasised by a golden lacquered glue by which the pieces are placed together. This way the vase or pot becomes even more valuable than the way it was before it was broken.

It is a beautiful metaphor people like to use to describe how difficult events in their lives that also broke them actually made them stronger, better, who they were really meant to be. Their pieces have been put back together and the work they used on themselves made the whole process gold. I also liked the idea except for one little detail.

I had never felt whole.

I have always thought there's some perfect, ideal way for me to be. That I'm not living my best life because I haven't found this world, I haven't cracked the code of how to free all my hidden energies. This wasn't something conscious, just a feeling deep down somewhere, buried under everything.

I have looked everywhere. I searched my heart and my mind. They guided me to beautiful places and lofty principles, and while I sat under the olive trees in the rosemary- and basil-fragranced late August evening, or read about truth, justice, and rights, I felt the world is beautiful, everything is perfect, and there's nothing wrong with me.

I fell in love with great cultures where there was peace, harmony, and order. My heart and mind were both drawn to a right way to live and to worlds where the sun is shining and wonderful flowers bloom in the most unexpected places.

I got immersed in worlds where people were together, lived in big families, there was love and laughter, and people were respected and accepted as they are. I thought if I do everything I'm supposed to, I will be treated with justice and my God-given rights will be provided. I saw values, I saw principles, I saw warmth, community, and family.

And then I found myself alone fighting for my basic rights.

What I hadn't seen was that the people conveying these lofty principles were broken inside. They never knew warmth, only a set of rules. Mercy and love were mere words for them. The whole system was broken, full of injustice, suppression, and compulsion.

The very same things I had tried to escape from for a long time before. Just like in the Steven King movie when the protagonist thought he was walking by the seaside, and he entered a post office but found himself back in the hotel he wanted to get away from but could not.

You cannot run away from your fears.

But at that time, I didn't know this. I wasn't ready to face them. I just wanted a life. I just wanted to be happy. So I searched for my utopia through escapism.

I came from a sad, brown and grey reality where I was alone. Everyone dealt with their own problems and there was no room for joy. Really, as I'm writing, I'm trying to grasp the essence of my childhood in Hungary, and perhaps this is the point. No joy, no laughter, no freedom. As if there was always something to be afraid of. Actually, my parents did grow up in fear and their parents feared for their lives.

It's quite enough reason for escapism I think.

But there's more.

Becoming someone else is a tradition in my family. Both my father's parents lived under altered family names in order to prosper, and then to simply stay alive. My mother's whole family had to leave their homeland where they had become foreigners due to political decisions. They didn't know their *mother country* was not their home, even if they spoke the same language.

This is Eastern European reality.

Little minorities being suppressed, exiled, killed, exterminated. Still, we are lucky it's not ongoing as in other parts of the world.

And if you happen to be the offspring of multiple minorities, you try everything to find your identity. To stay alive.

One of these survival tactics is to find someone from a stronger, more solid cultural background. Obviously, this as a *survival tactic* is totally unconscious; you just fall in love without asking for passports or listening to old family histories, but it happened more than once in my family. I did it, my father did it, my grandmother did it, and her father did it too, I don't know what happened before. It's not an outward thing, it's not to gain acceptance in the society; actually, sometimes it's quite the opposite. It's more like a deep desire to belong to a big clan where everyone has a safe place. The unexpressed desire for acceptance.

And then you will either need to give yourself up in order to be accepted or the whole system collapses. Or both.

Or the whole clan is exterminated. That can also happen.

Where do I belong? What is my real crew? Who are my people?

The pieces of the puzzle I'm put together from? Yes, I share things with many of them. A familiar pronunciation, words, foods, a way to look, to feel, to think.

It's nice, it's family. But they are not my home.

Or people I share the same principles with. Well, I do share the same principles with every good-willed person anywhere in the world, regardless of their cultural background. Moreover, the way of explaining mercy as compulsion, as, unfortunately, the majority of those I *share principles with* think, is not something I can sign up for.

Random soft-hearted people I met along my way? Yes, it's mostly them. But you meet and you say goodbye again and everyone goes home. Where do I go home to?

Where is my home?

I have always tried to belong to communities (only for some of them to let me down when I was at my lowest).

I learnt languages and researched cultures basically all my life. I saw all the beauty in them and everything that was missing from my life. I wanted to become one of them in order to possess those qualities I saw in them.

Oftentimes my views were biased, as if I looked through a pair of pink sunglasses. I saw the sunshine and not the clouds (if there were, it was *nice weather* for them). I saw the bright pink flowers and not the barren earth. I saw the beautiful historic houses and not the rubbish all around. I saw confident, educated women and not oppression and illiteracy. I saw openness and not backward customs. I saw lavender-coloured shadows but not the shadows of society.

Sometimes I feel it was a beauty inside of me that was lying dormant and undiscovered that finally found its shape in the colourful world I found.

I definitely needed my travels, they shaped who I am. I learnt new ways that felt much more natural and much more mine than those I was born and raised into. I gradually discovered how to be me. I learnt tranquillity, acceptance, kindness, trust, strength, confidence. I learnt that you don't need to be afraid. Trust God and do what you can. I learnt that it's much more than you had ever thought of.

This has always been my way. People say, 'You need to know your mother tongue, then learn the grammar of a foreign language, then you can learn to speak.' I did it the other way round. I learnt to speak again at the ages of 18, 19, 20, and 23. Perfected what I learnt at 19 when I was 28. And then even at 34. I was there expressing myself. Everything I feel. Everything I want. Everything I see. In new situations. Under new skies. Breathing a different air. Becoming a new me. The grammar always came after, having already acquired a new voice.

Or people say, 'You need to know your own country before you travel,' but I just couldn't do that. *My country paralysed me.* I couldn't speak, I couldn't walk, I couldn't breathe. It wasn't my home, I just wanted to get away to learn to live. So I did.

And now, having mastered the art of how to be, having meticulously picked the ingredients of this fruit salad of oranges and figs, brugnons, pomegranates, mangoes, and prickly pears, having absorbed all the vital vitamins from it, I'm ready to face where I come from.

I'm 45 years old. I have become an optimist in the sea of pessimism, open-minded among closed-mindedness, having questions where everyone has answers, active in the swamp of passiveness and strong where everyone around is playing the victim. I'm not bragging about it, there's nothing to brag about. It was decades of hard and painful work. I suffered, I stumbled many times, and it never looked like I was winning. But I always chose my path, the way of my sunny dreamlands over the sad and gloomy Eastern European swamp.

What broke me was that people from my dreamlands who came from the sun, those from whom I had learnt every human's innate rights, learnt how to be a perfect person, how to create a perfect family, perfect community, perfect society, neglected and denied my very rights. These people who came from the land of queens treated women as commodities. They used them only to serve their agendas, but as soon as they became too noisy or wanted some authority or simply their rightful minimum, they seemed to be treated as unwanted nuisances who had to be eliminated.

I didn't expect this. I had a barrier against the easily recognisable negativity, that which I grew up in, but receiving such treatment from a place that apostrophed itself as *those who live in peaceful harmony with the will of the Creator* was more than I could deal with. It was like becoming lonely again, just as I had been before when I lived in a society that was alien to me. It was like losing my family for the second time. (The first time it wasn't like a specific point, it just never happened that I felt protected and accepted.)

I found myself alone, having also lost the only person who really knew who I was, even during the time I seemed to forget it. The loss of my sister woke me up like an ice-cold bucket of water. I realised that life was not going to become a walk in the park just like that. The way to live was not by just sitting in the swamp and maybe one day it would become beautiful. I understood it could become terrible anytime. Anything can happen even to those most actively working on their healing. If I'm just sitting around, I'll be lost for sure. I had to be proactive to make my life better. That's how the greatest tragedy of my life has become my biggest wake-up call.

So there I was without personal support, without community support, but in my loneliness I finally understood the nature of my soul. Walking alone and contemplating the nature of how humans are put together, I was committed to freeing my soul. I listened to her cry and it was bigger than a baby's head. I lost my dreams, my security, my hopes. I told God, 'Here I am. Show me what's the point of all this.' And I started to actively love myself. The pain gradually started to shrink, and here I am; all the visible parts of it can be taken out of my body. Now I'm receiving a disinfectant cleansing treatment so that the possible microscopic dangers can be eliminated once for all.

And now I think I'm ready to look back. The sadness of my childhood doesn't scare me anymore. Eastern Europe is not a scary, oppressive place that wants to kill my soul. I don't feel it as threatening. I see it as a victim. Generations, centuries, even millennia of broken people hurting each other. Soulless zombies suppress others simply because that's the only way they have ever known.

Obviously, to feel this way I needed to know that I'm safe now. They cannot harm me anymore. I don't depend on that place, on that system in any way. And the other, equally important element is that I have already expressed my pain. Not everything. I believe there are still layers I wasn't ready to uncover yet, but what I had access to, I did listen to. I heard my soul's cry. I sat down with her and held her. Washed her wounds, cleaned her, and gave her new clothes. That of dignity. And I have placed her back to her rightful role, as the commander of my life. She is sitting on her throne right now dictating these words.

Without this process first, there's no compassion towards anyone hurtful, even if it wasn't intentional. Cheap forgiveness is no other but the diminution of one's pain – that's yet another attack against the soul. And I'll never allow anyone to hurt her anymore.

But once my soul is safely reinstated in her role, I can go to see what it was that hurt her. It's not only curiosity. It's important to face one's fears because as long as they are not addressed properly, people recreate similar situations with the deep, unexpressed hope that this time it will end better. But if we don't enter the situation consciously, we will keep on playing the same role in the same scenario, only the scenery is different. I can even go to Mars and surround myself with Martians, but if I haven't faced what really happened to me, I will be the down girl of Mars, playing the very same role of me trusting people just because I decided to, being patient with them because in my dreams they will care one day and then – wow, surprise! – losing everything.

What is this pattern anyway? Where did I get it from? Yes, my mother did the same. But why? Where did she learn it from? And all the women in her family before, throughout the centuries, who did everything to accommodate others and denied their own needs? Is it simply global patriarchism that every woman is a victim of? Or hurt people hurt people even more, meaning that in societies where everyone already suffers, the status of women is even worse? All of that is most probably true as this is the reality of women's lives in this and actually in most parts of the world. We can't really name any culture that is not patriarchal, and thus, female individuals suffered more and were subject to suppression, so it's a global phenomenon.

Or there are those who define power and strength as oppression, rudeness, and disrespect of others. They require power for themselves but at the expense of others' weakness. It's not sustainable and this behaviour only perpetrates tyranny. We can see a lot of *strong women* like that in Eastern European society, but I have never met a real strong woman there.

It's also something I had to go far away for, to see good examples, learn them, and make those ways my own. A strength that makes others strong too. A confidence that instead of living off others' weakness, respects them and considers them equal. A beauty that is not exclusive and not unique, but is as a single flower in a bouquet, allowing others to shine in their own ways. I learnt all that among Asian women, mostly Yemenis or Iranians. And again, this felt much more natural and *my way* than the Eastern European doormats or harpies I have seen growing up.

Only among two of my constituent nations, together they make up almost three-quarters of *me*, do I feel some deep, undestroyable force. One of these nations has lived in exile as second class citizens for more than 2000 years now, subjected to continuous persecution, hate, and hostility. There's no wonder they are broken, but it feels like an outside thing, the effect of what happened to them over the centuries. Inside, they are the radiant Middle Eastern women their ancestors were. My other *main constituent* nation is most probably related to Volga Bulgars or some Caucasian tribes. As these people gradually changed their language and forgot their origins, their deep, inner strength sank under the surface. But it's there, and when they manage to discover it, it shines bright like the sun, just like other Asian women.

This is the deep strength I found inside after having seen it in its pure form in other places. Real Mediterranean, Middle Eastern, and Asian women whose strength is not buried under centuries or millennia of Eastern European hostility and lethargy but shines bright as the sun. I learnt from them how to be me. And through this process, I believe I relive the hidden strength of my ancestors that had been buried for centuries under persecution and hate and under the compulsion to assimilate and hide their true characteristics.

Who am I?

A mixed heritage minority Eastern European woman? A traveller who has adopted the ways of interesting people she liked because she didn't find herself at her home? A single mother struggling with health issues?

I think I'm all of that. A mosaic of little pieces of the wonderful nations of my origins found broken and faded, but polished and given back its shine. And those of my travels, ways that came instinctively and willingly. All of that wonderfully glued together by the golden lacquer of my joyful, sorrowful, and even bitter experiences.

My medicine is my glue. It restores me as a whole after having been cleaned of the effects of suppression and hostility.

Love
31.08.2023

It was chilly this morning as I walked towards the bus. I was wearing my leather jacket (got from the charity shop in Maidstone last time – best place!), my pink loafers, matching pink–navy outfit, and my rose gold Ted Baker bag I got myself for my last birthday. I haven't worn it a lot though, maybe sometimes in London, but for chemo I decided I would always dress up. I really looked like a smart woman getting up early to go to some fancy workplace.

I was. Healing is my job now.

At the hospital, I got my horse riding helmet, or it may look like the one for bungee jumping (ice-cap), and my cannula – the second time the lovely nurse managed to insert it into my damaged vein. And then I got the water of life.

Nice 80s–90s music played in the background and a smiley lady was walking around offering tea and biscuits. Both the nurses (and by the way everyone I have met so far) were really kind and I felt I liked coming here to see these nice people. And even about the suffering part, the needles and weird feelings and stuff, I understood deeply in my heart that, essentially, it's love.

Everything that surrounds us is the manifestation of God's love towards us.

All that I went through the past year, the past 5 years, the past 45 years was there to get me here and beyond.

Last year I experienced my circumstances changing step by step, and along with that, I was changing too. And now I feel I don't only not need to worry about what will happen to me, but I also do not need to worry about myself, my own development. Mostly professional, that's what was in my mind as I was walking home between the lovely houses in my neighbourhood, but now as I'm writing, I realise it probably includes my health as well.

Since I had lost my job 2 years ago due to my health and my circumstances (I was in Hungary and couldn't make the phone calls to UK, and then I was not even able to concentrate on translations, let alone organising and multitasking), I knew that now I needed to heal, but somewhere in the back of my mind I felt I needed to be more productive. I don't exactly know if it was the internalised expectation of society or my restlessness about knowing deep inside I'm able to do something big – probably both – but to be able to do it, I needed to arrive here mentally, physically, emotionally, and spiritually. There's some kind of Native American saying that's said after some big, tiresome event: 'Now we sit down and wait for our soul to reach us'. This. I feel my soul has reached me, is now at its rightful place, and now I'm not afraid of the future. OK, let's say for now I'm less afraid. But it's getting better, really.

By the way, 2 years ago I was very productive. Important parts of this book were written at that time while I was in and out of hospital and walking around another therapeutic, wonderful town. I was working on my first opus while I was sharing what I understood, realised, felt, because I had to, It was a deep inner urge.

Everything around and inside me is one. This is also something new for me to realise. I have always felt somehow *left out*, felt I was different as a person, and my path in life was also definitely not ordinary. I actually never wanted to be; it's not only like I never could fit in, I never wanted to. I always wanted to find my own way.

I remember I was very young, maybe not even twenty, when my mother once told me I was self-contained. This translation doesn't give the full meaning. In Hungarian the wording is *having your own law* and it means something like you just follow your own path in a way that you don't really care about the rest of the world, and that's not necessarily positive. I felt sad as deep inside I wanted to follow God's law, but I haven't really found guidance on how to do it.

Then I found guidance that although it involved my heart at first too, it was more about mental and material laws. They were all important and also had a place in my path. But now I have arrived at the point that I can connect to God on a spiritual level.

My soul and my heart understood (in their own abilities) that I won't reach God if I compulsively follow rituals and worry if it's enough – if I'm enough – all by suppressing my inner voice – my soul. And how many people are doing it! My heart aches for them! They feel, they think, they are told that it's what God requires. Even if something breaks their heart and destroys their soul. 'To give up for God', that's what they are told. Even when what they are required to give up is their God-given right.

Unfortunately, it seems like the solely mind-way to reach God gives too much opportunity for suppression by people. They can twist and turn rules and explanations according to their own needs, and if we don't have our soul strong, they can destroy that too. All while 'there is no compulsion in religion' and 'Allah has breathed His soul into Adam, peace be upon him.' All the lectures are only about rights and duties (matters of the mind and body) and the other two constituents, the soul and heart, are completely neglected if not banned.

This is not bringing anyone closer to God.

How could you become more spiritual by crushing your spirit?

I have to add that it was not intended in the Quran, it's not what the Prophet, peace be upon him, taught. It is unfortunately what happened to many other religions and world views – people turned and twisted them in order for them to have a means to suppress people.

Anita Moorjani said her religion is love. I can relate very much to this. She also said religions are for this world for people to be guided, but they lack a lot of information and contain a lot of human influence.

I follow my religion, but not according to the way many people interpret it nowadays.

I don't deny my heart, I open it to perceive God's all-encompassing love, and feel that all that's happening in my life, and actually everything in this world, is the manifestation of His love. I also use my heart to channel that love to my dear children, family, friends.

I don't deny my soul either; on the contrary, I place it as my compass, my guide. It shows me all the things in this world that belong to me.

And about the laws? I follow them as much as I can – according to the teaching. Not *fear Allah* as much as you can, but rather *be God-conscious*, that's what the word *taqwa* means. Without fear of not being enough. Without feeling left out or less than.

To learn about my rights was crucial for me to know my importance and it made me stronger. Before that, I didn't know about it and I always felt weak in the Eastern European world that's designed to crush you. But when I understood that God created me with my unalienable rights, it helped me gain self-confidence.

Then those who taught me my rights deprived me of them.

Now I really feel strong and it doesn't depend on any outer factor. My strength comes from my unity with the world that's the manifestation of God's love towards us. I'm part of it. Not something small, not enough, not someone who needs to strive and suffer in order to attain it. I'm included in God's love. In fact there's nothing in this world that's excluded. It's the rahma we have talked about earlier. My strength comes from that.

I'm where I'm supposed to be. My life is exactly at the point where it has to be. This is my gift from God and I'm grateful for it. I recognise God's love and it lights up my heart.

And I believe I'm at the best place now and I'm led to many wonderful things – healing, love, and success.

I love you all. Thank you for having read my book.

When you shed your
Snake skin of
Trauma responses
And you become
Who you are
Really meant to be
Everything is possible

The author

Julia Tarjan was born in Budapest in 1978, in a
family of intellectuals of different cultural heritage.
Curiosity towards other ways of living, tolerance
and knowing different languages was the basic
atmosphere she grew up in.
Julia studied art and languages and worked as
a translator for many years. She was particular-
ly interested in the Mediterranean and Middle
Eastern world, Italy became her second home and
she also spent a year in Yemen studying Arabic
and immersing herself in the culture. Coming
back to Hungary, she volunteered as an activist for
cultural understanding, a task that had become
increasingly difficult in the political climate of the
country.
She moved to the UK in 2019.
Julia continued her studies in the field of mental
health and counselling. Today she writes, raises
her children and is healing from cancer.

novum ◆ PUBLISHER FOR NEW AUTHORS

The publisher

" *He who stops getting better stops being good.*

This is the motto of novum publishing, and our focus is on finding new manuscripts, publishing them and offering long-term support to the authors.
Our publishing house was founded in 1997, and since then it has become THE expert for new authors and has won numerous awards.

Our editorial team will peruse each manuscript within a few weeks free of charge and without obligation.

You will find more information about
novum publishing and our books on the internet:

w w w . n o v u m - p u b l i s h i n g . c o . u k